Lione

Snorkelling Manual

A guide to snorkel diving techniques for the use of instructors and pupils in the BS-AC National Snorkellers Club

Published by
The British Sub-Aqua Club

1st Edition 1974
2nd Edition 1976
Reprinted 1977
3rd Edition 1980
4th Edition 1982
5th Edition 1985

Acknowledgement is due to the following:
Illustrations: David Brown
Photographs: Lionel Blandford and Mark Jenkins

ISBN 0 9506786 0 0

Printed in England by Eyre & Spottiswoode Ltd, Thanet Press, Margate

Contents

Introduction

The National Snorkellers Club was inaugurated in January 1974 as the official junior section of the British Sub-Aqua Club, and superceded the Snorkellers Award Scheme which had started in 1970. In the ten years since its formation, over 22,000 children in 380 branches have been enrolled in the NSC.

The first edition of this manual was produced in 1974 for members of the NSC by its Director, Lionel Blandford. Successive editions have updated and improved the communication of snorkelling techniques for new members. Each of these editions and this the 5th edition have also been authored by Lionel. Lionel as an advanced club instructor of the BS-AC, as a teacher for the Royal Lifesaving Society and as the Director of the NSC, continues to devote his energies and enthusiasm to the training of children in the sport of underwater swimming. Members are taken through a progressive course of training to become highly qualified snorkel divers from the Junior Snorkeller Award to the NSC Advanced Instructor.

The incredible popularity of the National Snorkellers Club means that there is a continual demand for more and more instructors and branches to cope with the number of children anxious to learn to snorkel dive. Because of this, Headmasters and Youth Officers encourage their staff to take NSC Instructor Training Courses and to start their own branch.

The NSC organise snorkelling holiday courses twice a year in the Mediterranean and the islands around Britain. These holiday courses are open to all children aged 11 to 16 years and are extremely popular. Staffed by top instructors and with a qualified nurse in attendance, a full course of safe instruction is provided in ideal conditions in the sea.

As the present Chairman of the BS-AC I would like to express our continued thanks to Lionel, not only for producing and updating this manual which will help to introduce so many more people to the joys of underwater swimming, but also for his untiring efforts which have made the NSC such a success. The progression of many NSC members to full membership of the BS-AC is an added bonus.

Information on all matters relating to the NSC can be obtained from The Director, National Snorkellers Club, 13 Langham Gardens, Wembley, HA0 3RG.

I. A. N. Irvine
Chairman, British Sub-Aqua Club

Foreword by H.R.H. The Prince of Wales President of the British Sub-Aqua Club

As an occasional and very amateur diver I am delighted when an authoritative book is published which will encourage others to learn the basic principles of the sport with maximum safety.

This book is designed for young people making their initial steps – or fin strokes – in learning to snorkel, first in a swimming pool, and then in the open sea. The principles embodied in this book have already been used by the British Sub-Aqua Club National Snorkellers Club to train over 10,000 boys and girls in safe snorkelling.

It is important for young people to have a leisure interest and when that interest not only gives pleasure, but imparts a sense of self-discipline and responsibility, I know that they will gain qualities which will benefit them throughout their lives.

I hope that what they see and experience when snorkel diving will encourage them to progress later to diving with an aqualung, in order to enjoy the underwater world to the full.

Charles.

Author's Introduction

The fascinating films of underwater exploration being produced in ever-increasing numbers, never fail to capture a vast audience of spellbound followers, both young and old. Thrilling scenes of intrepid skindivers wearing highly technical and expensive equipment gliding gracefully through the rotting remains of stately galleons carry the entranced viewers deep into the realms of fantasy. But with the end of the film comes the swift journey back to reality and the unhappy conclusion by the uninformed that this is a sport exclusive to the wealthy and the fictional world of cinema and television.

But the awe-inspiring beauty of the

Lionel Blandford

No expensive equipment is required to stake a claim in this new dimension because all that is needed is a mask, fins and snorkel. However, this is just the beginning, for, as in all sports, to get the best result, it is necessary to learn the rules. Snorkel diving is no exception for the sea is a mighty power imposing very strict rules indeed. So, to enjoy your snorkel diving, and above all, to snorkel safely, a rigid course of training must be completed before venturing into the sea. This manual has been produced in the hope that it will prevent your enjoyment being marred by incidents due to lack of knowledge about the sport and ignorance of the hazards that may be encountered. Primarily, this manual was for the use of members of the BSAC National Snorkellers Club and the first edition was a sell-out due to the phenomenal growth of the Club. The second edition included a chapter on Marine Biology to assist the many members to progress even further in the sport. I am indebted to Dr. David Bellamy—the renowned Marine Biologist and television personality—for 'vetting' and approving the chapter. Dr. Bellamy requested that I stress the importance of conservation and the prudence in the taking of specimens. I am more than happy to comply with Dr. Bellamy's request for I, too, want to go on enjoying the beauty beneath the waves. I already know, from the many letters received, that the young snorkellers of the world will support this request and willingly form a junior army of conservationists to defend and preserve the life in the sea. A chapter on ropemanship was included in the third edition to assist snorkellers to become capable and efficient in all aspects of the sport. I have also included a section on snorkelling games and contests for the benefit of the numerous snorkelling clubs which use this manual as their training guide.

I welcome suggestions of additional information or comments for the improvement of this manual. Extra games suitable for snorkel divers will be most welcome as well as constructive criticism.

This edition updates the manual with minor alterations but the programme and tests remain the same.

Preparing to Start the Adventure

It does not matter whether you intend to learn to snorkel dive with a friend or to join a snorkelling club in order to do so, there is one essential requirement. Any would-be snorkeller must have a high degree of stamina and be able to swim reasonably well. It is sometimes thought, quite wrongly of course, that because it is comparatively easy to propel yourself along with fins, it is not necessary to be a good swimmer. But if a weak swimmer were to lose a fin, and it is quite easy to do so, there could be serious consequences.

This is the reason why, when you join the National Snorkellers Club—and this is by far the best and safest way to learn to snorkel dive—your training begins with a rigorous and progressive course of free swimming. In fact, the NSC Swimming Test was formulated to ensure that prospective

Briefing

divers have sufficient swimming ability and watermanship before commencing snorkel training. This manual is only intended to cover snorkel diving so there is no attempt to offer any instruction or hints on swimming. However, if you propose to learn the sport of snorkel diving without joining a club you should commence by improving your swimming to the NSC Snorkeller Award standard which is as follows:

1. Swim 200 metres front stroke.
2. Swim 100 metres back stroke.
3. Swim 50 metres wearing a $2\frac{1}{2}$ to $4\frac{1}{2}$ kg weightbelt (according to build).
4. Float for 5 minutes.
5. Tread water for 1 minute.
6. Dive 6 times to minimum 2 metres and bring up a brick each time.

Members of the NSC take the Junior Snorkeller badge course to assess their ability before continuing with the actual Snorkeller Award course. The junior course is as follows:

Swimming (no equipment)

1. Swim 50 metres front stroke.
2. Swim 25 metres back stroke.
3. Float for 1 minute.
4. Hold breath for 15 seconds underwater.

Snorkelling (with mask, fins and snorkel)

5. Fit equipment correctly.
6. Fin 50 metres on front.
7. Fin 25 metres on back.
8. Perform 3 competent surface dives.

Upon completion, pupils are awarded the Junior Snorkeller badge and continue training for the Snorkeller Award badge and certificate.

The start of the lesson

The Choice of Equipment

Before you can commence your snorkel training, you will have to purchase your basic equipment. this should be done with the utmost care because it is necessary, in the interests of comfort and safety, to have the right type of gear. Therefore it is advisable to buy the equipment from a shop specialising in diving gear and where an experienced diver can ensure that you are correctly equipped. The casual selection from the seaside arcade shop is not recommended as the range of equipment is not usually extensive. Also there could be a possibility of you being sold items which are not only the most expensive, but which are totally unsuitable and possibly dangerous.

The Mask

Let us consider, first of all, the Diving Mask. The human eye, unlike that of the fish, was never meant to function efficiently under water. Consequently, when the naked eye is immersed in water, the vision becomes blurred. In order to obtain vision under water similar to our normal vision, it is necessary to have an airspace between the eyes and the water. This is the reason for the diver's face mask.

The Mask

However, owing to the higher refractive index of water, the wearing of a diving mask under water causes objects to appear one-third larger than they actually are and so they appear nearer. Whilst this is misleading at first, the diver soon becomes accustomed to it and, as experience is

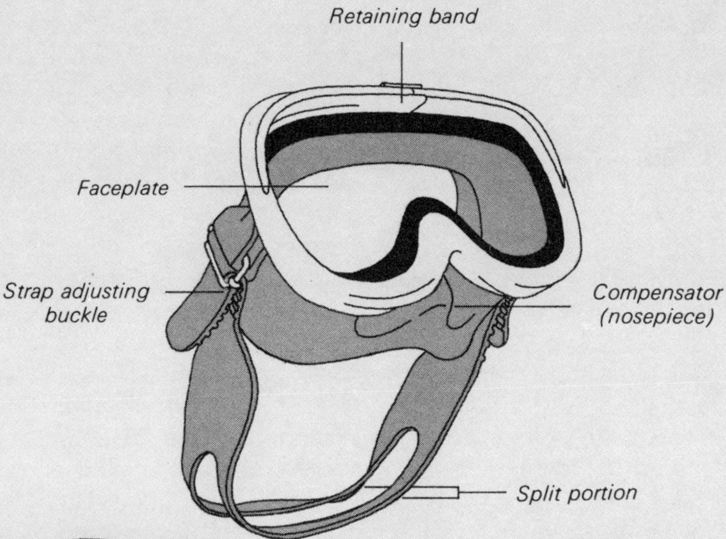

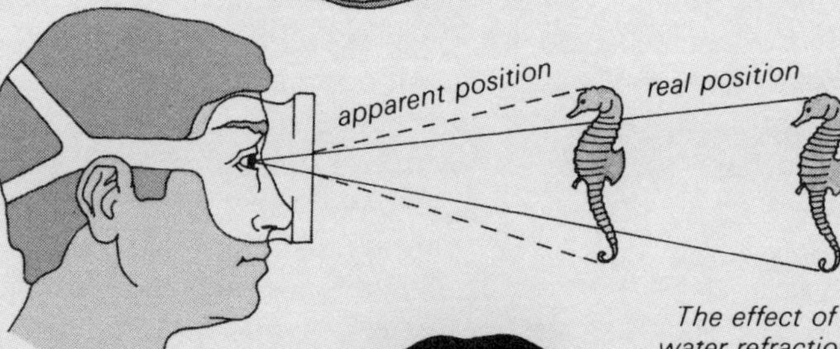

The effect of water refraction

Testing for fit

gained, is able to make the necessary allowance for it.

It is preferable for your mask to be fitted with safety glass rather than perspex. Although the latter is safe, it mists up considerably more than glass and also scratches easily. If you look for the word 'Toughened' or 'Tempered' on the face plate, you will know that it is not perspex.

If possible, choose a mask with feathered double sealing on the edges of the 'skirt' and with the glass secured firmly in place with a metal or plastic band. Double or split straps are advisable and in order to maintain the required tension, there should be a firm locking device. Metal parts should be non-corrosive and the rubber should be soft and resistant to chlorine and salt water.

The mask should only cover the nose and the eyes and a compensator (shaped nosepiece) is essential for 'ear-clearing' which is explained in a later chapter. A drain valve is optional and does, in fact, make mask clearing easier but this refinement obviously increases the cost and is an additional possible cause of leaking. Under no circumstances should you select a mask with a built-in snorkel as these can be very dangerous owing to the possibility of rebreathing the carbon dioxide-contaminated air in the face mask. A full face mask is unsuitable for snorkel diving and is designed for use primarily by commercial or service divers. Goggles which only cover the eyes must not be used because it is not possible to equalise the pressure as the nose is not enclosed and therefore no air can be breathed into them. This also means that air cannot be used to clear water from them should they become flooded.

To try the mask for fit, push back the hair and place the mask on the face without securing the straps. Breathe in through the nose and if the mask fits correctly, it will be sucked on to the face and stay in position until air is expired from the nose. When fitted, it should be comfortable and not too heavy, provide good clear vision and be completely watertight. Make sure that the straps which hold the mask in position are adjusted correctly—not too loose or too tight because either way could cause leaks. It is not possible to wear spectacles with the normal diving mask but it is possible to get a special mask with optical prescription lenses to give proper vision under water.

The Snorkel Tube

The second piece of equipment which a snorkel diver needs is a snorkel tube. This enables you to keep your face under water and still breathe normally whilst surveying the scene below. The simplest form of snorkel—an ordinary 'J' or 'L' shaped tube—is by far the most suitable and efficient. It is preferable for the snorkel to be made of rubber or flexible plastic although it is possible to obtain one made of aluminium. These metal snorkels can be

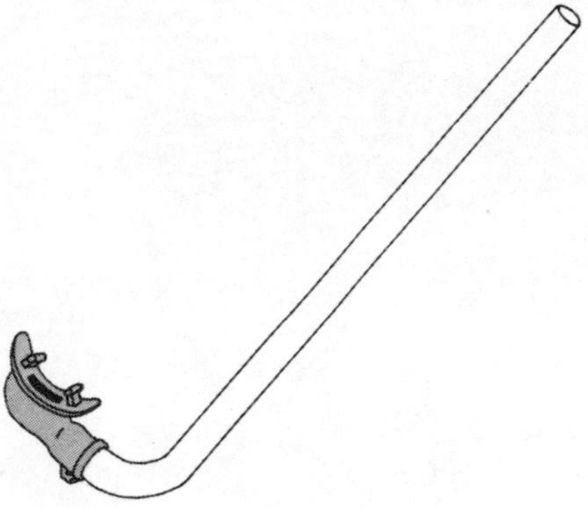

A typical snorkel tube

dangerous to your 'buddy diver' as they are quite sharp and they can also be easily dented causing the air supply to be obstructed.

The snorkel should be 30-35 cm long. If it were any longer, it would cause serious problems. The reason for this is that it is physically impossible, due to the water pressure on the body, to inflate the lungs sufficiently at a depth of a metre or more. The problems of pressure are dealt with in a later chapter however. The inside diameter of the snorkel tube should be 15-20 mm. A smaller inside diameter would restrict the air supply to the diver and a larger one would result in considerable difficulty in clearing the water from the tube.

Snorkels should not be fitted with a valve as these can be dangerous. If the valve jammed in the open position, there could be serious consequences. In addition, valves on snorkel tubes only operate when the tube is in an upright position and unless the tube was kept upright throughout a dive, it could become flooded. This could cause a beginner to panic if a lungful of water was sucked in due to the valve failing to close.

Under no circumstances should a snorkel be fitted with an attachment utilising a table tennis ball. The ball could become distorted under pressure and stick inside the tube. The National Snorkellers Club has been very active with regard to the standards of snorkels and masks in an attempt to improve them. These efforts have been successful and British Standards Institution Specification BS 4532 has now been amended to ensure maximum safety and efficiency.

The Fins

Let us now consider the next piece of equipment for the snorkel diver . . . the fins. Before choosing them, you should fully understand their function. Basically, their purpose is to provide you with a larger lever with which to push against the water and so propel yourself along. They are in fact, an extension of your feet and increase the thrust thus enabling you to manoeuvre more effectively and with the minimum of effort. (Maximum propulsion with minimum effort).

As the hands are used for other things such as handling a camera or examining marine specimens or other underwater objects, a snorkel diver depends mainly on his fins to control his movements and move through the

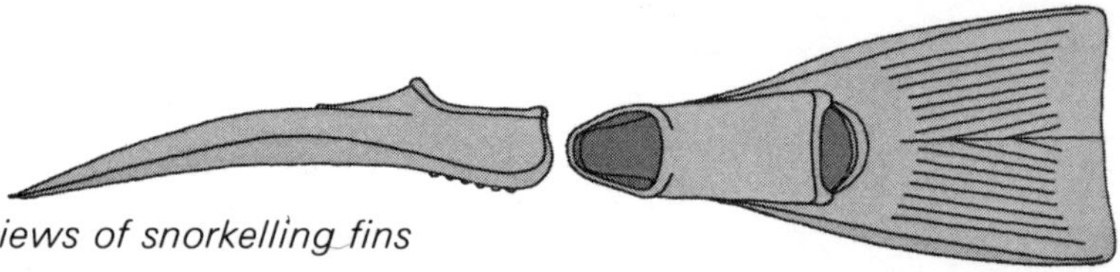

Two views of snorkelling fins

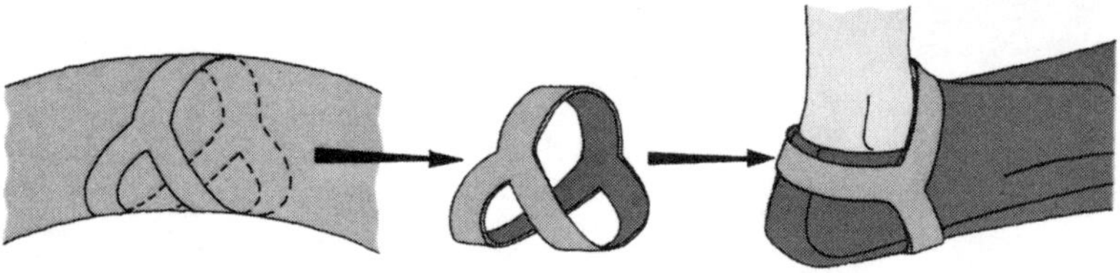

Fin retainer cut from an inner tube

water. This is why they are such a tremendous asset in life-saving as the arms are left free to hold and tow the subject without losing any power of propulsion.

There are two main types of fins—the open heel type with an adjustable strap and the full shoe pattern. The former are satisfactory for very young snorkellers as the straps can be adjusted to allow for growing feet. They are, however, not so comfortable as the shoe type and the straps have a tendency to slip and break. The full shoe pattern is therefore preferable for the snorkel diver.

The fins should be manufactured from good quality material, the blades kept firm with strengthening ribs and the shoe part moulded with a softer rubber for comfort and ease of putting on. The blade should be angled so that when the legs and feet are fully extended, the fins assume almost the same straight line as the legs. Avoid fins that are too loose and 'floppy' as they will cause blisters and serve little purpose, but conversely, do not get them too tight as this could cause dangerous cramp. Floating or non-floating fins are a matter of personal preference. Floating fins have a tendency to keep the feet too high causing the legs to thrash the surface of the water and splash excessively but they have the advantage of returning to the surface should they be accidentally knocked off during a dive. Generally speaking, aqualung divers use non-floating and snorkel divers use floating fins. If you intend wearing a wet suit with bootees (Neoprene Socks) it is necessary to have either a separate pair of fins or to buy them two sizes larger. In this case, you will, of course, need to wear the bootees in your fins even when swimming in the pool. As an additional precaution, a pair of fin retainers can be worn to hold the fins more securely. These can be made very easily by cutting a 'Y' shape from an old motor cycle inner tube as shown in the illustration

Young snorkeller kitted up

Using Your Equipment

Now that you have your basic equipment, you are ready for your first attempt at snorkel diving. This may present a problem as unfortunately, many swimming pools do not permit snorkelling during the normal public swimming periods. This is because it may cause inconvenience to 'free swimmers' and therefore, you may find that the opportunities for using snorkel diving equipment are limited. The easiest, and the safest solution is to join a branch of the National Snorkellers Club. This is because more and more local authorities have come to appreciate the importance of safe training and are making swimming pool sessions available for the exclusive use of branches of the NSC.

Your training at an NSC branch would start with the correct use of your equipment and you would first be shown how to fit your mask. To prevent it misting up, give the safety glass a good wash inside and out with 'soggy' soap powder to remove the 'film' that is usually present on a new mask. Prior to use in the pool, always spit on the glass and rub the saliva around it. Then rinse it without wiping. This appears, somewhat crude, but nevertheless, it is the best way to prevent misting inside the mask. Other demisting aids are raw potato or seaweed.

Before putting the mask on, it is a good idea to cool the face with cold water as a hot face can cause the face plate to steam up. Place the right hand over the face plate of the mask and position the strap over the back of the hand. Clear the hair from the face with the other hand and then place the unobstructed facial contour (skirt) of the mask in position on the face. Breathe in slightly through the nose—this should hold the mask in place—and at the same time pull the strap backwards over the head with the left hand to the correct position at the top and back of the head. *Do not put the strap on first*. Ensure that the straps are adjusted tight enough to provide a good seal around the face to keep the water out but not too tight so as to be uncomfortable in use. Remember that it is now only possible to breathe in through the mouth although you can, of course, breathe out through either the mouth or the nose.

Now enter the water. It is preferable to lower yourself in or to go down the steps but if you do decide to jump in, don't forget to hold your mask in position.

Look under the water with your mask just below the surface and see how clear everything appears. Then try swimming along with your face plate half in and half out of the water. When you have perfected this, you will realise that you can see in front of you and also below without moving your head.

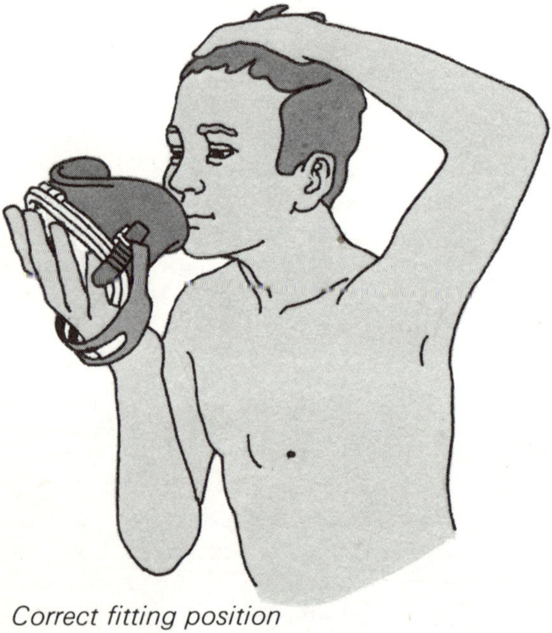

Correct fitting position

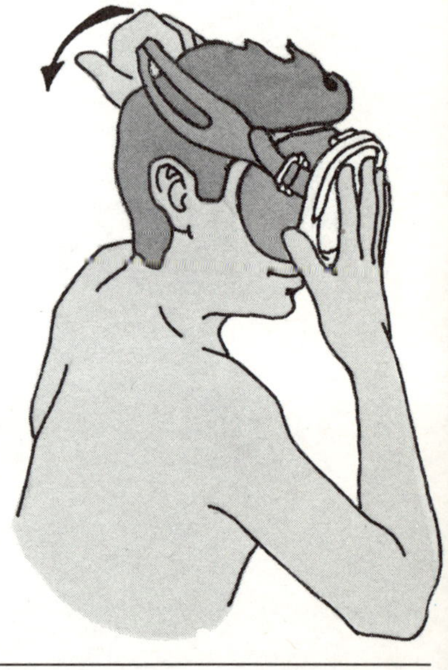

You are now ready to try the snorkel tube. Gently pull the mask strap sufficiently away from the side of the head to allow for the straight end of the snorkel to be eased under the strap immediately in front of the ear. Care should be taken to ensure that the snorkel tube does not lift the mask from the face and cause it to let in water, so, if necessary, loosen the strap a little to make allowance for the tube. Make sure too, that if your snorkel has a right or left deflection, it is inserted on the correct side of the head. As a guide, it should be as near to upright as possible when the face is looking down and slightly forward.

Grip the snorkel mouthpiece lightly between the teeth—it is important not to grip the mouthpiece too tightly as this only results in an aching jaw and possibly biting off the teeth grips on the snorkel mouthpiece.

Duck your face just below the water and practise breathing through the snorkel tube. If you duck your head under too far, the tube will naturally take in water, so practice is necessary in order to maintain the correct depth.

If water does enter the tube, it is a simple matter to give a sharp 'putt' to clear it. This can be made easier still if you tilt your head towards the snorkel side so that the water in the mouth-piece flows back into the tube before you clear it.

right
Correct head position to clear snorkel tube

below right
Incorrect head position

below
Correct head position when finning

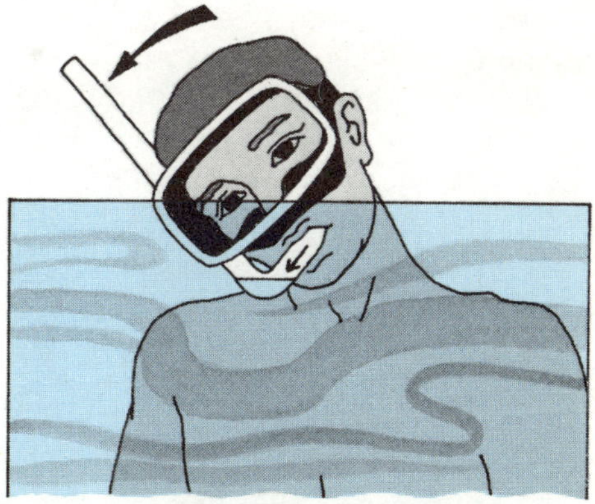

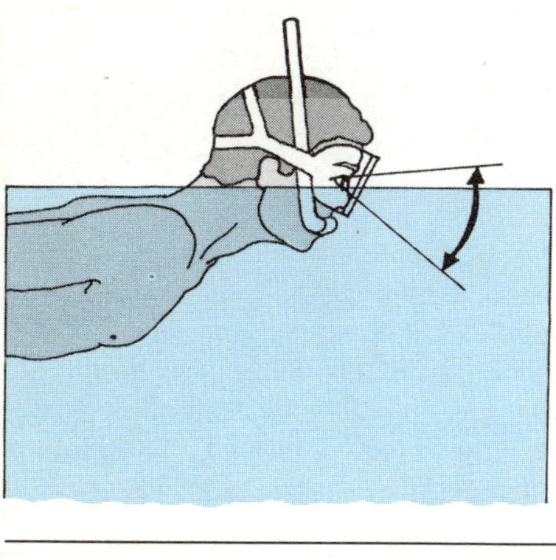

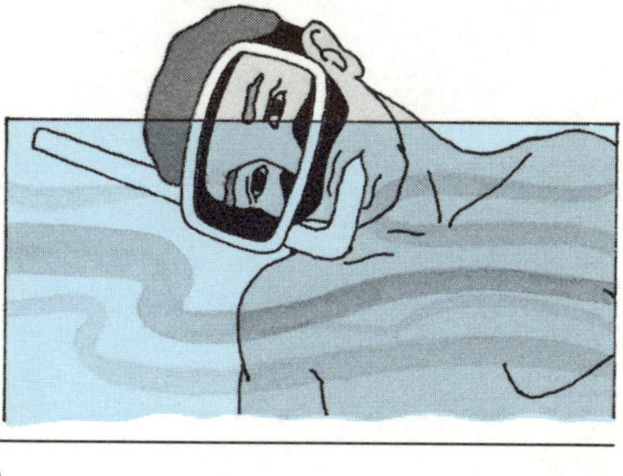

Now try swimming with the mask and tube in position, occasionally allowing water to enter the tube and 'putting' it out again without swallowing any. Concentrate on breathing in and out through the mouth and try to completely forget that your nose exists. Don't forget that when you 'clear' your tube, the water will shoot backwards so make sure that you do not have your back towards the unsuspecting onlookers at the side of the pool. They will not be amused if a jet of water from your snorkel saturates them.

The next stage in the process of learning to use your equipment is to try using the fins. Place your mask and snorkel on the side of the pool and then wet the fins. Turn the heel part inside out and put the fin on the ground. Kick the foot into the shoe portion holding the fin by standing on the blade portion with the other foot. Then flip the heel part into its normal position. Repeat the process with the other fin and walk backwards carefully down the steps into the water. Take care to place your feet well on to the tread of the steps as the fin blades will not hold your weight.

Hold on to the handrail round the pool with the left hand and lay flat on the water. The arms should be stretched out with the right hand pressed against the side of the pool under the water with the fingers spread and pointing downwards. Keeping the legs stretched out and the toes pointed, commence moving them up and down using the hips as a pivot. At first, keep the knees stiff and ensure that the fins do not break the surface of the water. After some practice, it will be possible to relax and very slightly flex the knees to assume the correct finning action to give maximum propulsion through the water.

You should now be ready to try snorkelling with the full basic equipment so retrieve your snorkel and mask from the poolside and refit them correctly whilst remaining in the pool with your fins on. First, try a couple of widths of the pool at the shallow end using only your fins to propel you and keeping your arms alongside your body. Look ahead with your back slightly hollowed and your legs down to avoid thrashing the surface with your fins. If you find difficulty in keeping the legs down, clasp your hands behind your back, lift your head clear of the water and recommence finning. Should this method still fail to produce the desired result, remove the mask and snorkel, clasp the hands tightly behind the back thrusting them well down on to the seat and resume finning with the head and part of the chest held high out of the water. When you can keep the fins down, you can replace your mask and snorkel.

Practice your finning until you have mastered the technique but beware of relaxing too much and adopting a 'cycling' action which is tiring and provides very little thrust. A good finning action provides maximum propulsion with minimum effort.

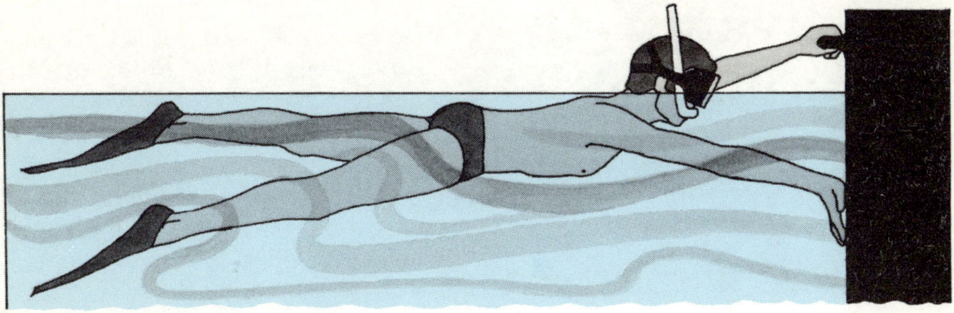

Learning to fin correctly

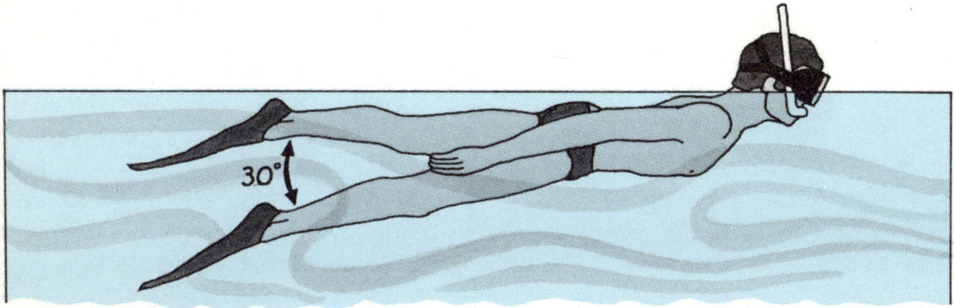

Correct finning position

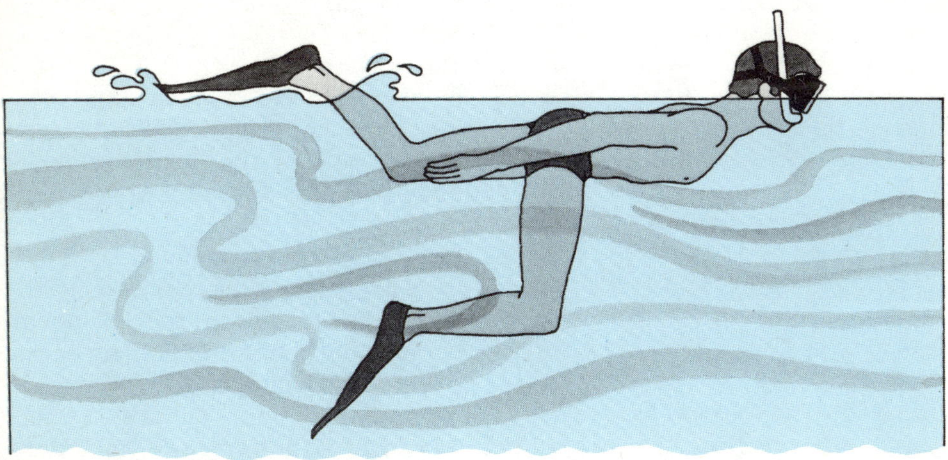

Wrong—cycling action

Improving Your Performance

Now that you understand the basic snorkelling techniques, it is time that you progressed to more advanced manoeuvres. Up to now, you have been entering the pool down the steps but it may not always be possible to do so. You can take your choice from four methods of entry into the water and the first is the step-in entry.

To perform this entry, you just take a big step from the side of the pool. At the same time, you must place your right hand on your mask with your thumb under the snorkel mouthpiece. Your left hand should be positioned on your left side—the reason for this is to get you used to holding on to your weightbelt which you will be wearing in the future. Step straight forward with the right leg and allow the left leg to collapse so that you drop straight into the water. Do not remove your hands from their positions until you are under water and remember to clear your snorkel when you surface. Be sure to step in and not jump.

The second method is the push-off entry and this is self-explanatory. You just sit on the side of the pool with your hands on the edge and push yourself feet first into the water.

Rolling-in is the next method and this involves keeping the legs completely stiff with the head tucked down towards the knees. Holding the backs of your legs with your hands, you just roll forward into the water. You should be able to manage this quite successfully without holding the mask.

Methods of entry

The surface dive

The last method is rolling-in backwards. You simply sit on the side of the pool with your back to the water with your knees pulled to your chest and roll backwards into the water. Keep your arms clasped round your knees and your head tucked in until under water. When you have mastered these methods of entry into the water, your are ready to advance your knowledge and snorkelling ability.

Finning on your back is quite exhilarating as you can develop astonishing speed. You have to keep your chin on your chest and pull your snorkel tube towards the front of your mask to avoid flooding it. In the pool or calm water, however, you can remove the mouthpiece from the mouth altogether. Finning on your side is a restful variation as long as you make sure that your snorkel is on the uppermost side.

There will be times when you will want to dive down to examine something so you should know how to surface dive. This must be performed with the absolute minimum amount of splashing so as not to disturb or frighten the object which you wish to examine more closely. To carry out a surface dive, fin towards the deep end of the pool and when you are ready to dive, drop the upper half of the body straight down with the arms pointing to the bottom. Lift both legs together straight up in the air and at the same time sweep the arms back in a wide breast stroke. Whilst the weight of the legs equipped with fins should be sufficient to drive the body downwards, the arm stroke will expedite the manoeuvre and the body will glide rapidly downwards through the water. Remember to take in sufficient breath for the dive and retain enough to enable you to clear your snorkel on surfacing.

Going down

Another method of surface diving is the feet first method. This is performed from a vertical position in the water and involves giving a powerful vertical finning action to lift you high out of the water. The arms can be held in a horizontal position and pushed down as you rise to give added thrust. Keep the legs close together and the arms by your sides and your weight will carry you down. Once under the surface, you can move off in the direction you wish to go.

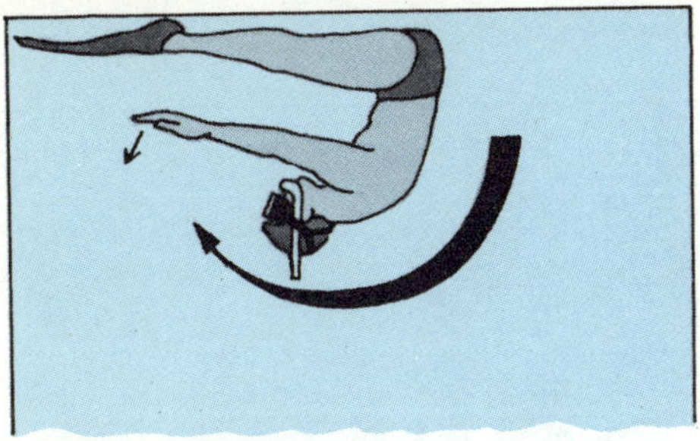

The forward roll

When you have mastered both kinds of surface dive, you should then attempt forward rolls. The starting position is the same as for a head first surface dive but the arms should be kept close to the sides. Drop the upper half of the body and instead of keeping it in a vertical position, curl it round and draw up the legs to form yourself into a ball taking care not to bend the knees. Sweep the arms forwards and downwards with the palms scooping the water backwards to propel the body in a somersaulting motion. As only the arms are used for propulsion, it is important to apply equal pressure with each arm to avoid rolling sideways.

The backward roll

Backward rolls are performed by finning on the back and then ducking the head and arching the back. At the same time, extend the arms above the head and sweep them forward to assist the body in a somersaulting movement. Once again, as with the forward roll, equal pressure must be applied with the arms and it is a good idea to follow a line on the bottom of the pool to ensure that you are keeping straight. The legs should be kept together throughout the rolls.

Whilst practising the various manoeuvres, you may experience flooding of your mask and be forced to stop and clear the water from it. When you eventually start snorkelling in the sea, you would find it a nuisance if you had to keep stopping to clear your mask so you should practise mask clearing under the water. This is really quite a simple operation and will enable you to clear a flooded mask whilst finning along under water with no effort at all.

First, take a good breath and with the aid of a weight belt to keep you down, kneel on the bottom of the pool. Lift the top edge of your mask slightly to allow the water to seep in. Now look up so that the faceplate of the mask is at an angle of 45° to the surface and press the top edge gently on to the face without distorting the mask) and snort out through the nose. This will have the effect of filling the mask with air and forcing the water out at the bottom. When you have mastered this, practise it whilst finning along under water, remembering always to look up as you do so.

Mask clearing

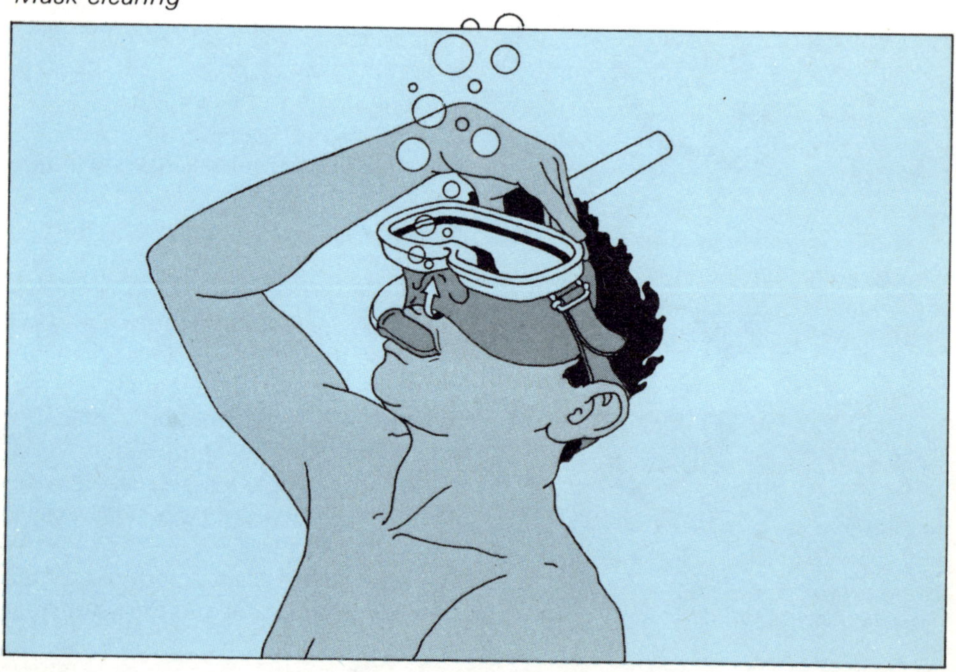

To improve your technique even further, try removing your mask completely, replacing it and clearing it whilst still at the bottom of the pool. You will soon find yourself clearing your mask without even thinking about it which will be a big help should you knock your mask against a rock or another diver accidentally kicks you with his fins. Concentrate on using as little air as possible in this exercise or you will have to come up quickly for air and this will defeat the object.

You should now practise fitting your basic equipment in the water. Sink your fins, mask and snorkel in the deep end of the pool then surface dive to recover one piece of equipment at a time and fit it on whilst treading water. It is not important in which order you retrieve the items but you may find it better to recover your mask first as it will make it easier to see the other items of equipment. Do not try to dive from the treading water position as this is a waste of energy and more difficult. It is better to fin away a little and then approach and perform a correct head first surface dive. If you have floating fins place a weight belt on them at the bottom before diving to retrieve them.

When you are diving in the deep end of the pool, you should start practising the correct procedure for surfacing in the sea. As you come to the surface, look upwards circling as you do so and look in all directions. Raise your hand above your head as you break the surface and give the OK signal (described in the next chapter) with your arm straight up in the air. The raising of the arm above the head has another purpose besides signalling and that is for protection. On a sea dive, there is always the possibility of surfacing under an overhanging rock or a boat and getting an unpleasant bang on the head. It is far better to graze the knuckles than to knock yourself out or risk severe head injury.

You should take every opportunity to practise snorkelling because it is the only way to develop your technique. However, as with all things, self-tuition has considerable limitations and an experienced instructor will possibly be able to correct faults of which you are not aware. Make enquiries at your pool to find out if there is a qualified Snorkel Instructor there or better still, find out where the nearest branch of the National Snorkellers Club meet and go along and join.

Divers' Signals

It is very important that divers are able to communicate with each other and with their boat cover or the shore. Without very expensive equipment, it is impossible for them to talk to each other under water so an international code of hand signals has been devised for communication. Snorkel divers do not need to know all of these signals but some of them are very important and should be thoroughly learnt and understood.

All underwater signals should be given clearly and deliberately, using the right hand where possible and always in front of your face mask. Make sure that they are understood and acknowledged by your buddy diver. When signalling to the shore or your boat cover, signals should be given with the right arm extended to make sure that the signal is seen and acknowledged. Generally, only signals (j) and (k) on page 29 are used with the arm extended as the other signals are mostly used between divers in the water.

Figure (a) shows the signal indicating the person or thing referred to in the signal that follows—viz. you, me, him or it. Figure (b) is the most important signal because it is used to enquire 'Are you OK?' The reply is either the same signal indicating that all is OK or the signals shown in Figure (c) 'something is not quite right' or Figure (d) 'Help me, I am in trouble'. Figures (e) and (f) are for going up or down and Figure (g) is an indication of the direction to proceed in. The flat hand used in the signal in Figure (h) is directing you to stop or stay where you are. All these signals should be learnt and practised with your buddy diver until they become second nature to you.

All 'OK'

DIVERS' HAND SIGNALS

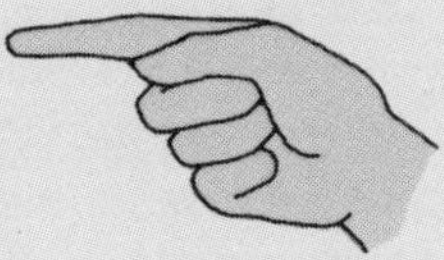

a) 'The person or thing referred to'

b) 'OK all is well'

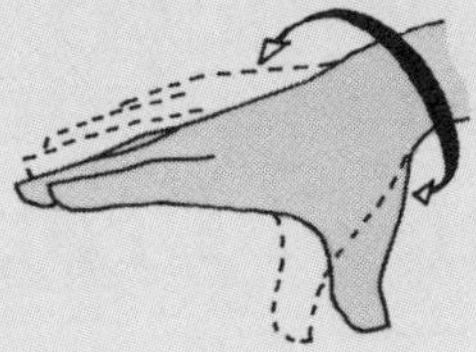

c) 'Something is not quite right'

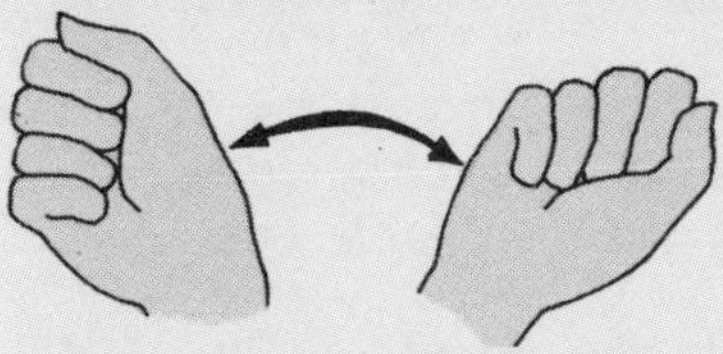

d) 'Help me, I'm in trouble'

e) 'Go up'. 'I am going up'

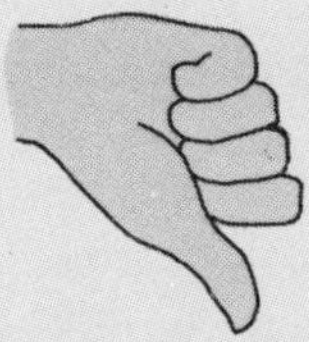

f) 'Go down'. 'I am going down'

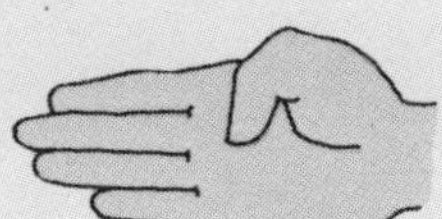

g) 'Let us go that way'

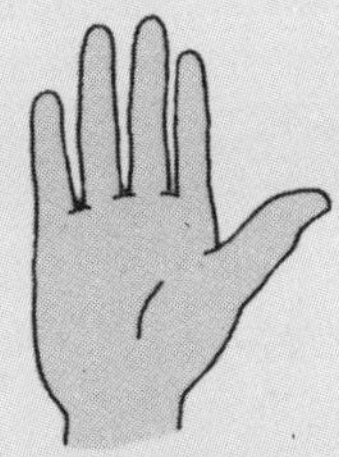

h) 'Stop'. 'Stay where you are'

SURFACE SIGNALS

j)

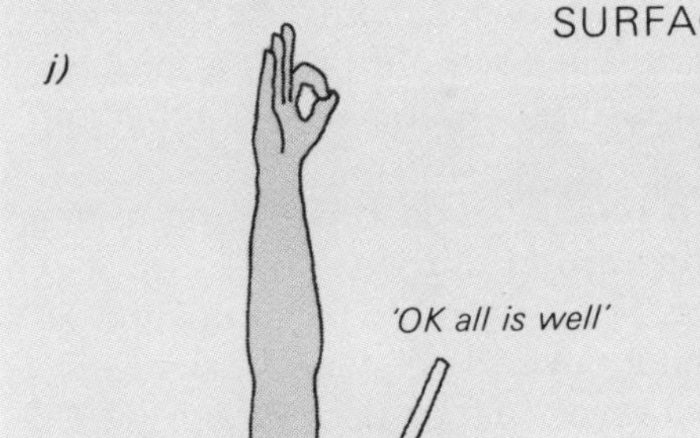

'OK all is well'

k)

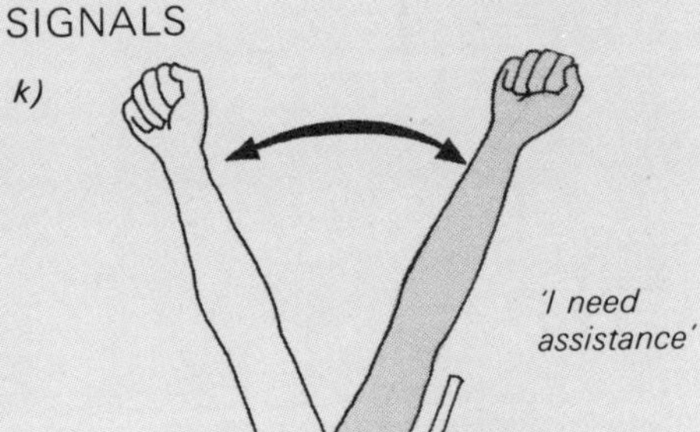

'I need assistance'

Advanced Techniques and their Problems

Whilst breath-holding competitions are dangerous and are to be avoided at all costs, it is important for divers to have good lungs to enable them to stay under water for a reasonable time. There is no fixed requirements but certainly 30 seconds should be possible after very little practice.

The best way to achieve this is by practising underwater swimming in the pool and aiming for a 15 metre minimum distance. Just take two good deep breaths before you submerge and fin along under water. Some divers allow air to trickle out very slowly from the side of the mouth. This eases the pressure on their lungs and enables them to complete their swim without that 'I'm going to burst' feeling. When you do try to hold your breath for 30 seconds, take in two good breaths and hold yourself under the water by gripping the steps. If possible, look around and observe what is going on under water to take your mind off the task in hand and again, allow the air to trickle out slowly from the mouth. By this means, you will never run into the problems caused by excessive deep breathing.

This repeated deep breathing to flush the carbon dioxide (CO_2) out of the system is called hyperventilation and must never be practised because it is extremely dangerous. When the CO_2 in the blood builds up to a certain level, it sets off a 'trigger action' to the brain which induces the stimulus to breathe. Other 'trigger actions' are a lack of oxygen and an insufficient

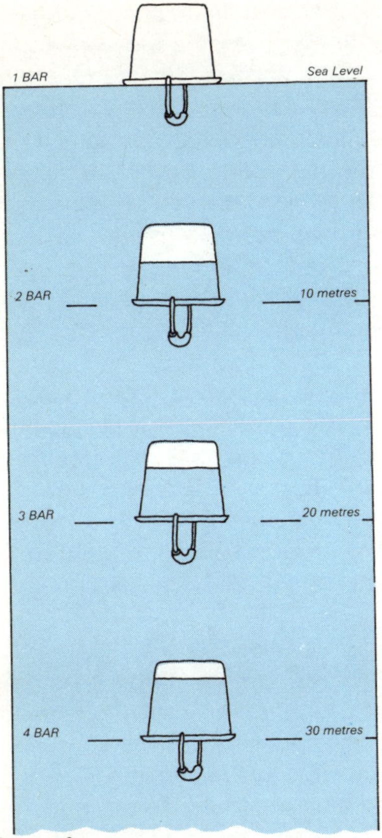

Effect of pressure

volume of air in the lungs. If the CO_2 is flushed out of the lungs, the diver could hold his breath so long that he uses up more oxygen than the body can safely afford to lose before the warning is 'triggered off'. Consequently, because the brain relies on a permanent supply of oxygen, a complete lack of oxygen (called anoxia) for even a few seconds could have a very serious effect and would certainly result in a black-out which in itself could prove fatal in the water. SO *NEVER* HYPERVENTILATE!

Diagram of Ear

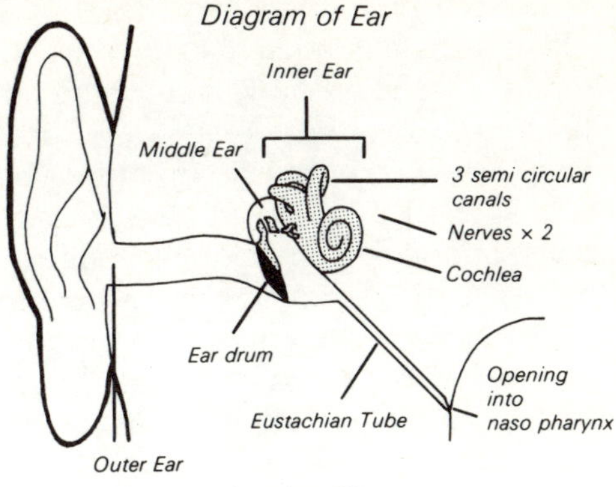

Diagram showing Sinuses

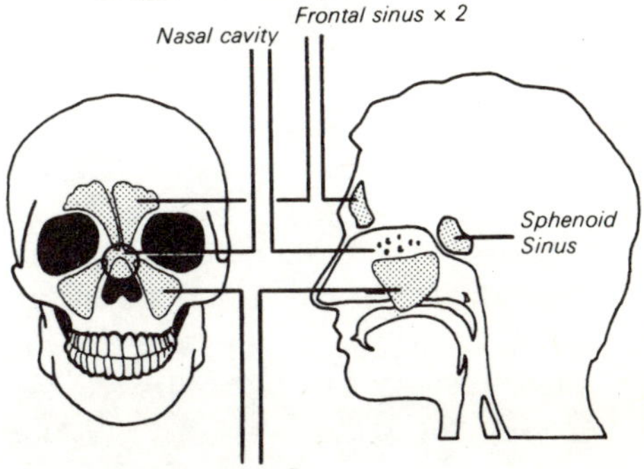

If you have been practising your snorkelling in a deep pool, you may have noticed a drumming or slight pain in your ears when you dived deeper than usual. This is a warning signal and must never be ignored. It indicates that the pressure on the outside of the ear drums is greater than that on the inside making it necessary to 'clear the ears' to equalise the pressure.

To understand this better, it is essential to appreciate the effect of pressure as we dive deeper. Our bodies are already subjected to pressure at the surface because the atmospheric pressure at sea level is equal to 102 kN per metre² (14.7 pounds per square inch).

This pressure is equally exerted in all directions and the body is accustomed to it so it does not create any problems. However, if we go up or down, we experience a different pressure and consequently have to make adjustments. Going up means less air pressure and a consequent drop in oxygen content with the possible need for an additional oxygen supply. But as we are only concerned with the effect of pressure when diving, we need only consider what happens when we go down.

For each 10 metres of depth in the sea, an additional pressure of 102 kN per metre^2 which is termed 1 bar (or 1 ats) is exerted. Therefore, at a depth of 10 metres, the body is subjected to an actual pressure of 204 kN per metre^2 (102 kN per metre^2 for the surface pressure plus 102 kN per metre^2 for the 10 metres depth).

It is this constant pressure which is used to operate a diver's depth gauge. It must be remembered however that as the pressure at the surface is 1 bar or 102 kN per metre^2, the gauge must be calibrated to allow for this. It should also be noted that fresh water is slightly less heavy than sea water and therefore the pressure is less—about two and a half per cent.

The human body is remarkably strong and being composed of fluids and solids which are almost impossible to compress, it will in fact stand pressures equivalent to more than 300 metres of depth. Unfortunately, however, certain air spaces within the body—in the middle ear and the sinuses—contain air and unless the air in these cavities is at the same pressure as that exerted on the rest of the body, pain and possible damage will result. This is the reason why you experienced the pain in your ears when you dived rather deeply in the pool.

The middle ear is connected to the back of the throat by the Eustachian tube. This is a very thin tube which is normally closed at the throat end to prevent germs from entering the middle ear. By exerting a slight pressure, the tube can be opened to permit the introduction of air which will equalise the pressure.

This 'ear-clearing' is achieved by swallowing or yawning, or by pinching the nostrils firmly, closing the mouth and steadily blowing on the nose. This will open the Eustachian tube and send air into the middle ear with an accompanying hissing or a 'pop'. If you have a cold, the tube may be blocked with mucus and you will be unable to clear your ears. This is the reason why you should not dive if you have a cold. It could be very dangerous to force open the tube as germs may enter the middle ear and set up an infection or, worse still, you could burst an ear-drum.

Should you force air together with mucus up the Eustachian tube to equalise the external water pressure, you could cause a blockage in the middle ear. The danger would then be on returning to the surface. As the outer pressure reduced the trapped air in the middle ear would expand and as its normal exit down the Eustachian tube would be blocked, it would go to the weakest point, the ear-drum. This again would cause pain and could cause the ear-drum to burst outwards which is known as a 'reversed ear'.

Ear clearing should be performed repeatedly during a dive and with practise, it will be carried out automatically without thinking about it. You should now appreciate why it is important to have a mask with a compensator (nose-piece) built into it. The sinus cavities are interconnected by passages to the nose and throat. Normally they are open and need no action to clear them, but again, in the event of a cold, they may be blocked by mucus, in which case, a severe pain would be experienced in the forehead. Therefore you should *never* dive if you have a cold. Swimming or finning on the surface does not normally worsen a mild cold so long as the body and particularly the head are dried thoroughly before dressing in warm clothing. The greatest problem is usually going home without thoroughly drying the hair, especially after a hot shower.

Another effect of the increase in pressure as you dive deeper, is an unpleasant sensation known as 'mask squeeze'. This is when the pressure of the water forces the mask on to the face and can result in bloodshot or black eyes on return to the surface. This effect can be counteracted by exhaling from the nose into the mask. It should be obvious from all this that nose-clips should never be used. Ear plugs are also dangerous because they could be forced deep into the ear. As you dive the air in the space between the plug and the ear drum would be compressed. On returning to the surface, the air would expand and could force the ear-drum inwards causing pain and possibly a burst ear-drum.

Rescue and Resuscitation

Assuming that you have thoroughly learned and practised the technique of snorkelling, you should be well on the way towards being a competent snorkel diver but never make the mistake of thinking that you know it all. There is considerably more to it than we can possibly hope to teach you in this manual and most of it will be learned by your own experience and continual practice.

Remember too, that snorkel diving is not a game and neither should you practise it alone. It is a serious and skilful sport to be enjoyed by two or more sensible people who should be capable of assisting each other or somebody else in difficulty in the water. This is why it is extremely important that you should learn life-saving techniques and Expired Air Resuscitation known as E.A.R. However, we must have a basic knowledge of the respiratory system to understand the principles of E.A.R.

Respiration (breathing in and out) is the means by which oxygen, which is essential to life, is taken into the body, together with the other gases in the atmosphere, and passed out again. Approximately 21 per cent of the air we breathe is oxygen and the remaining 79 per cent is composed mainly of nitrogen with minute quantities of other gases too small to really take into consideration.

The body is composed of millions of separate cells and in order to live and grow, each needs a supply of food and oxygen. This supply is maintained by the blood, carrying oxygen and food products, being pumped round the body by the heart to the capillaries where the tissues reject carbon dioxide and replace it with food and oxygen. The carbon dioxide is expelled from the body when it is returned to the lungs and breathed out in the expired air. The blood then extracts a new supply of oxygen from the newly-inhaled air and continues the process all over again. The nitrogen in the air breathed out is the same as breathed in but 4 per cent of carbon dioxide has been added to the air. This, of course means that the volume of oxygen is reduced by this amount so there is only 17 per cent instead of the original 21 per cent.

From these figures, it is seen that we breathe out at least four times as much oxygen as the body has actually used. Therefore there is still enough oxygen in our expired air for it to be used by another person and still satisfy the oxygen requirement. This then, is the principle of E.A.R. which can be performed on land or in the water. However, E.A.R. is only for use in an emergency as the body needs pure air to function correctly. Shortage of oxygen (hypoxia) can cause blackouts, decreased efficiency of the body cells and ultimately, complete lack of oxygen (anoxia) resulting in death. The most satisfactory method of administering E.A.R. in the water is the mouth to nose method as it is easier to obtain a complete seal over the nose. As this is most important and

Inspired

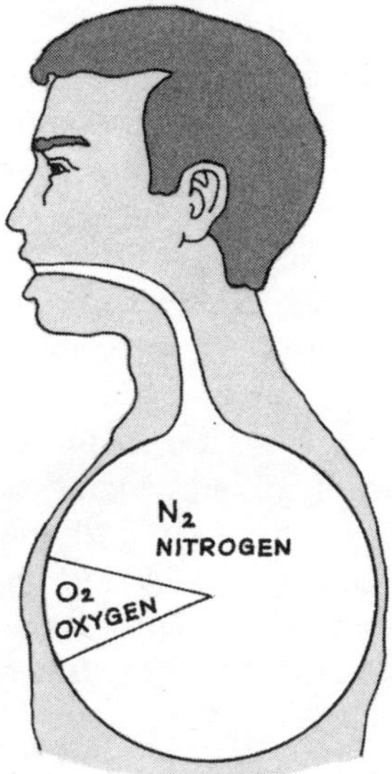

A

Expired

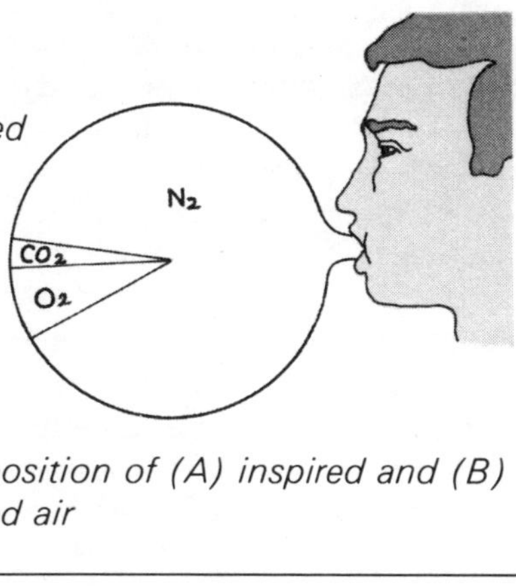

B

Composition of (A) inspired and (B) expired air

may have to be accomplished supporting an unconscious person in the water, it is well to practise it with a partner on dry land. Whilst practising E.A.R., it is more hygienic to breathe out alongside the subject's nose rather than into it. On dry land it is preferable to give mouth to mouth E.A.R.

Place your partner flat on the ground with a coat or a pair of fins under the shoulders so that the head is tilted right back to open the throat completely and keep the tongue from obstructing the air passage. Pinch the nose of the subject firmly with one hand and place your other hand over the chin to open the mouth. Now open your mouth wide and place it completely over your partner's mouth and give four breaths in quick succession. If air enters the stomach, you will notice a swelling at the bottom of the ribs, so gently press down on it to push the air out, then continue giving one breath every five seconds. This should be continued until the subject recovers or a doctor arrives. In practise you should blow on the back of your hand and not the mouth.

In an actual emergency, recovery is often accompanied by the subject wanting to be sick. At the first signs of vomiting, roll the subject sidewards facing away from you and clear his mouth and throat with your finger. It is most probable that breathing will have commenced but if not, replace your subject flat on the ground and resume giving E.A.R. When recovery has taken place, it is very important for the subject to be taken to hospital in case there are any after-effects. Before being taken away, and, even on the way to the hospital, it is best for the patient to be kept in the 'coma' position. The best way to accomplish this is to lay the patient face down on the ground. Draw up one of the legs so that the thigh is at approximately 90° to the body. This will cause the body to be half turned on to the side which will make it easier to extend the arms and bend them at the elbows and place them palms downwards alongside the head which will be facing the same way as the legs.

Once you are familiar with this procedure, you can practise an actual rescue. Before swimming out to attempt a rescue in the sea though, there are numerous factors to be taken into consideration and the handbook 'Life Saving and Water Safety' is well worth reading. This book, published by The Royal Life Saving Society covers all aspects of life-saving, including releases from the powerful clutches of a drowning person. As the subject of life-saving occupies the entire book, you will appreciate that we can only go into the subject briefly in this manual and therefore only consider the methods of rescue and resuscitation applicable to snorkel diving.

When attempting a rescue, it is obvious that you must get there as quickly as possible, but at the same time, you must not arrive exhausted as you could become a casualty yourself. Endeavour

Administering expired air resuscitation on land and in water

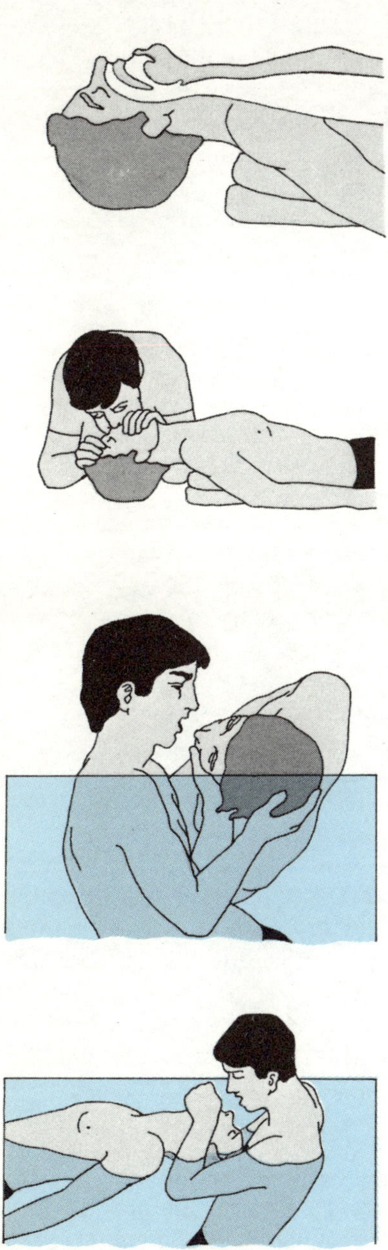

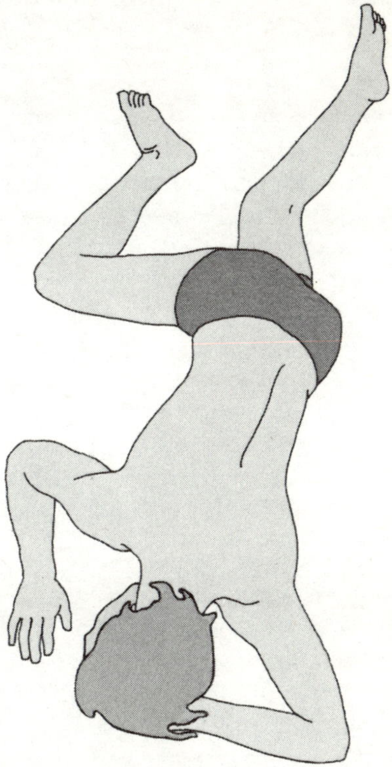

Coma 'recovery' position

to approach the person from behind so as to avoid being seized but if the subject is unconscious, commence giving E.A.R. immediately.

There are several methods of giving E.A.R. all with their relative merits, but experience has shown that the following method has proved most successful not only in training but in actual rescues in choppy water. Immediately you arrive on the scene, bring the unconscious person to the surface. Working from behind, place your left arm around the subject's left arm and your hand under the armpit—this hold ensures that your elbow pins down the subject's arm, then fin straight up to the surface with the subject slightly above you.

Use your right hand to sweep the mask and snorkel backwards over the subject's head with your hand finishing up supporting the head. Place your left forearm over the subject's left shoulder with your hand over the mouth and chin. Whilst finning slowly alongside in an upright position to keep above water, press down with your left elbow and roll the subject sideways towards you. Remove the mouthpiece of your own snorkel but leave the snorkel in your mask strap and commence E.A.R. making sure that you do not twist the subject's neck.

Using this method, you will find that it is not necessary to hoist yourself out of the water as the rolling action will bring the subject's nose round to your mouth with very little effort. A variation of this procedure is to retain the hands in the same position but to position yourself behind the subject's head and to press your left forearm against the collar bone to act as a lever. By this method, you are able to raise the subject's body horizontal on the water with the head well back and the nose in position to receive E.A.R. directly from behind with the minimum of upward finning required.

In both cases, the subject should be given four quick breaths and then taken in tow using one of the following methods which have been developed by the National Snorkellers Club (with minor variations) specifically for rescuers using fins.

Method 1 is used when it is necessary to keep a firm hold on the subject. The rescuer keeps to the left hand side with the right arm around the back of the subject's neck so that the head is supported by the upper arm with the forearm over the shoulder and down the subject's right side.

The left arm is positioned over the subject's left arm with the hand under the armpit. The subject's arm is stretched out sideways and pinioned by the rescuer's elbow. Holding the subject firmly and laying horizontally in the water, the rescuer can then begin to tow backwards. The rescuer should retain the mask but will find it easier not to use the snorkel.

Method 2 is used when assisting a subject who is tired or cramped but is prepared to co-operate with the rescuer. First of all, the subject should

Method of rescue—single handed (1 & 2) and when two reserve divers are involved (3 & 4)

Method 1

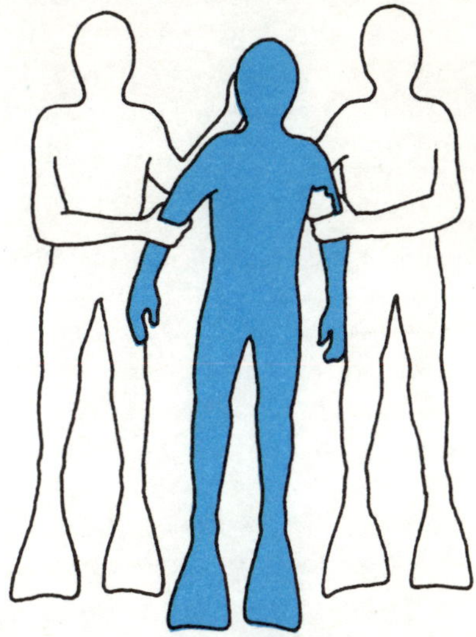

Method 3

Method 2

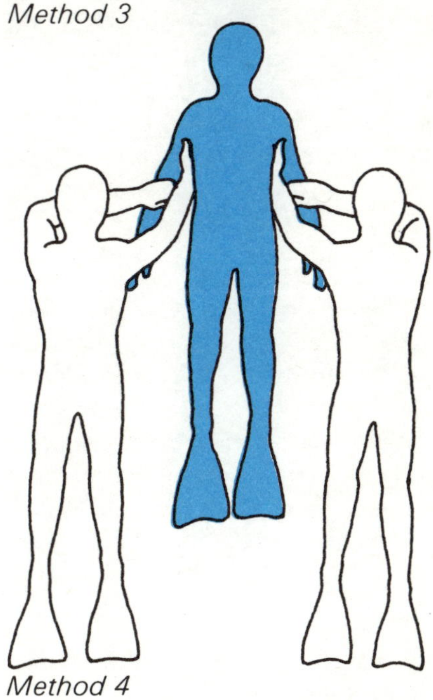

Method 4

lie horizontally in the water face uppermost and relaxed. The rescuer should fin forwards pushing the subject, whose arms will be grasped just above the elbows and held straight in front of the chest with the palms facing upwards. Both pairs of arms should be kept straight to ensure that the subject is under full control.

When there are two of you to rescue an unconscious subject, method 3 is recommended. One of you should place your right forearm across your body and hold the subject's right arm at the elbow with the right hand. The left hand should be used for supporting the head. The subject should be held close almost shoulder to shoulder. The second rescuer positions himself on the other side putting the right hand under the subject's left upper arm and gripping the lower arm with the left hand. Once again, a shoulder to shoulder position is assumed and with both of you lying horizontally in the water and finning backwards, you tow the subject between you.

Finally, method 4 is used when there are two of you rescuing a co-operative subject as in method 2. In this case, however, both of you swim along, one of you on each side, with the subject lying face upwards in the water. Both rescuers stretch out their arm nearest to the subject to obtain a hold under the armpit. The other hand is used to hold the wrist.

With the initial part of the rescue accomplished, the next thing is to get the subject out of the water. There are two methods of doing this and you should know and practise both of them. After all, if, on reaching a boat or a vertical bank, you were unable to get the subject out of the water, you would have problems. In shallow water, providing the subject is able to give assistance, you can use the stirrup method.

In this method both you and the subject face the bank with yourself behind the subject. Clasp your hands together and cup them under either of the subject's feet and hoist upwards on to the bank.

If the subject is unconscious and unable to help you, you should use the straight arm lift. With this method you lift the subject out of the water until the chest is resting on the bank. Press one hand on the subject's back to keep him from sliding back into the water and use your other hand to swing the subject's legs up on to the bank. This method can be used with a heavy subject.

Keep practising these methods and although they may sound complicated, take them step by step and practise them until you are really proficient. There may come a day when you, not to mention the person in difficulties, will be thankful that you took the trouble to learn how to save a life.

If you have practised regularly and have mastered all the techniques, you will be ready to take the NSC 'B' Test

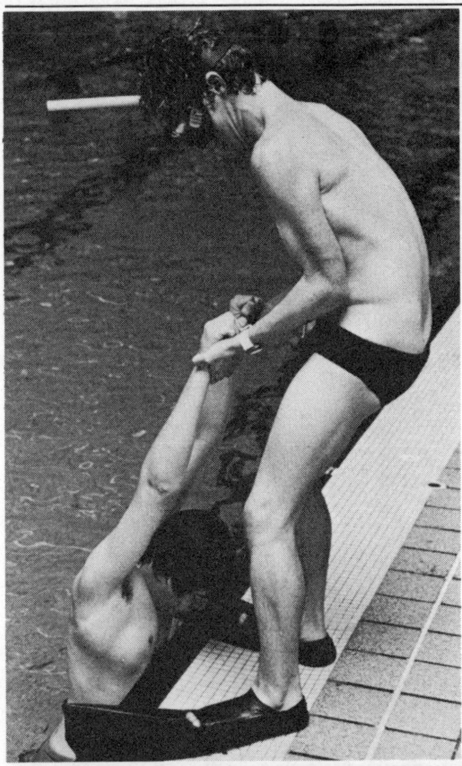

Landing Drill

for snorkelling. This test is to assess your ability to use the basic equipment correctly and effectively; to show that you have good snorkelling technique; and also that you are able to cope with different situations. If you are not in the NSC but would like to see whether you could pass the test, go along to the pool with your buddy diver and try to carry out the following successive tests:

1. Sink all basic equipment in the deep end of the pool at a minimum depth of two metres, then surface dive for each item in turn and fit it at the surface without support.
2. Fin 200 metres, surface diving every 25 metres.
3. Perform 3 forward rolls.
4. Perform 3 backward rolls.
5. Hold breath for 30 seconds underwater.
6. Fin 15 metres underwater without a snorkel.
7. Tow an adult (or someone at least as big as yourself) 50 metres using an N.S.C. method which incorporates E.A.R. in the water and administering it at least two or three times during this distance.
8. Land the body and continue E.A.R. on the poolside.
9. Carry out method 2 (tired swimmer assist) for a minimum 100 metres.

When you can complete them all with no difficulty, you will know that you can pass the test with no problems, but if you find difficulty or it is a struggle to get through them efficiently you should continue practising until you can carry out the entire test with the minimum of effort.

The Final Stages

In one of the early tests, you had to swim 50 metres with a weight belt on. It is now time to try finning with it. You should find this quite easy so now take it off in the water, place it carefully on the bottom and then surface dive to pick it up and put it on again whilst treading water. Always make sure that you have a quick release buckle on your weight belt and frequently practise 'ditching' it—but don't just drop it for it could wrap round your fins. Release it and pull it well clear of the body before placing it on the bottom. Do be careful to place it *gently* on the bottom because you would be very unpopular indeed if you dropped it and caused damage to the pool tiles.

You should now try finning 50 metres with your face submerged and without your mask. Use your snorkel tube for breathing and keep one arm outstretched in front of you for protection as you may have difficulty in seeing. If you do have problems, try it with a flooded mask or holding your nose but you must get used to breathing in through your mouth and out through the nose. Or alternatively, you can try it with your eyes closed and opening them as you fin along until you can eventually manage it with your eyes open.

Now get your buddy in the pool with you and with only one snorkel tube between you but both wearing masks, fin along sharing the same snorkel tube. Take two breaths from the snorkel then pass it to your buddy

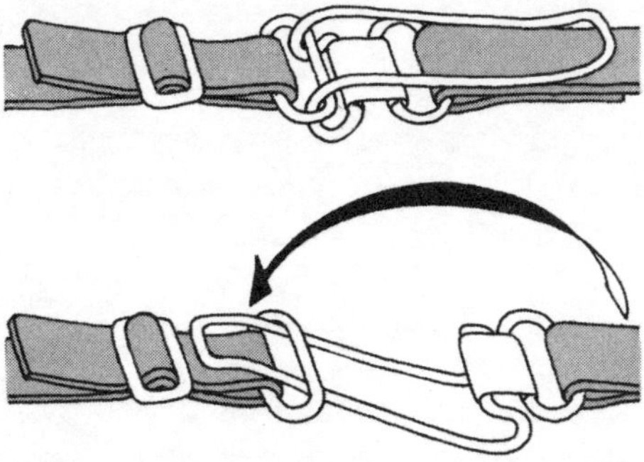

Quick release buckle on weight belt

who first puffs out to clear the water and then takes two breaths before passing it back to you to do the same. Get into a steady rhythm, finning casually and you will find that it is really quite easy. It is also a marvellous exercise for improving your breathing and ensuring that you always clear your tube before breathing in. In fact it will become second nature to you to always puff out when you put a snorkel tube in your mouth.

After all this training, you should be quite a proficient pool snorkel diver and if you belong to a branch of the National Snorkellers Club, it will be time for you to take the NSC 'C' Test. This is the final test to check stamina and ability to cope with conditions which could lead to exhaustion. It also ensures that you are able to control the air passage between the nose and throat. The six separate parts of the test must be carried out in succession without resting or taking any support and are as follows:

1. Fin 50 metres wearing a weight belt (maximum 4.5 kg but this can be adjusted according to build).
2. Release weight belt in deep end and remove mask. Place them on bottom of the pool.
3. Fin 50 metres face submerged using snorkel tube but no mask.
4. Complete (3) at deep end, retrieve and replace mask. Then surface dive and recover weight belt and refit in the water without support.
5. Give the signal 'I am OK.'
6. Fin a further 50 metres wearing the weight belt together with the mask, fins and snorkel.

When you have successfully completed the NSC A, B and C Tests, you can be regarded as a proficient pool snorkel diver but never let up on your practising, for a good diver keeps fit and competent at all times and *never* takes chances.

You will certainly need to be fit if you intend snorkelling in the sea. You will also need some extra items of equipment. Firstly, you will require a wet suit and in the next chapter, this is covered in greater detail. You will also require a weight belt with sufficient weight to counteract the extra buoyancy provided by the wet suit but remember that as you go down, you lose buoyancy so don't over-weight yourself. Make sure that the belt has a quick release buckle and that you can 'ditch' it with a quick flick of the hand.

You should wear a knife in a sheath strapped to your leg. Ideally, it should be fairly heavy with a thick stainless steel blade with a serrated edge. The knife is very important for cutting ropes and lines which could entangle an unsuspecting diver. You will often find abandoned fine fishing lines around piers which are almost invisible and which can sometimes be quite dangerous.

It is important that the knife has a serrated edge as it is very difficult to cut even a thin rope under water—it is necessary to saw it. The knife is, of course, useful in many other ways and

A diver's watch and a depth gauge which although essential for the aqualung diver are useful items of equipment for the snorkel diver.

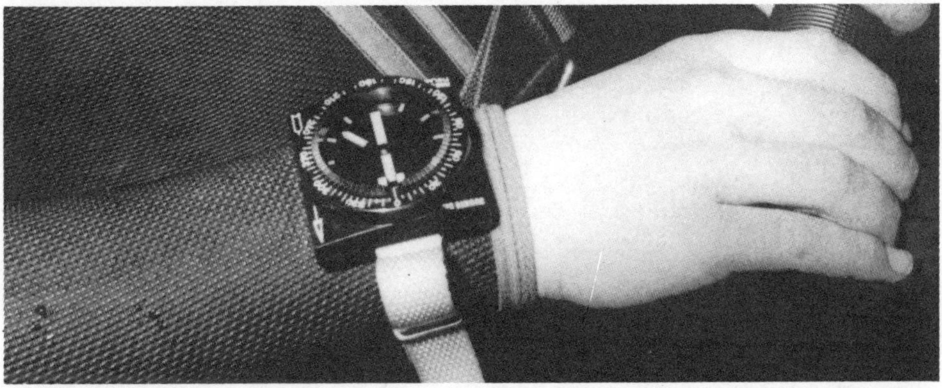

Both snorkel and aqualung divers rely on a compass for direction finding during diving.

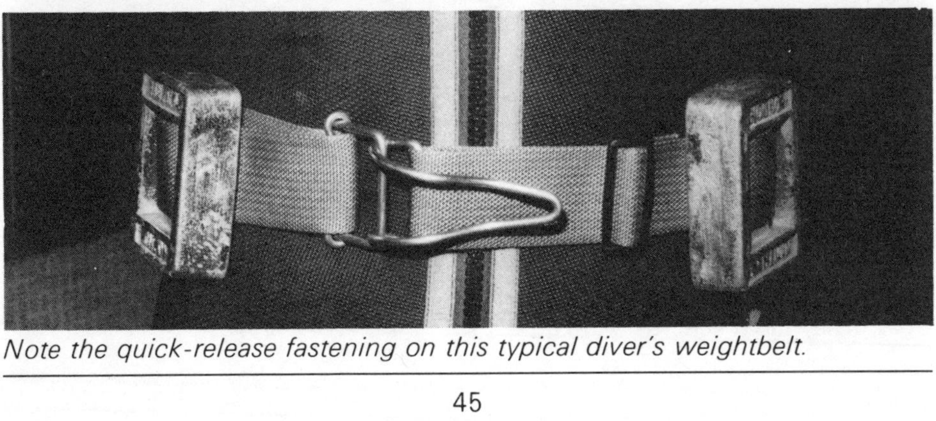

Note the quick-release fastening on this typical diver's weightbelt.

should be cleaned and greased regularly as the salt water affects the blade even though it may be made of stainless steel.

You will be well advised to buy a life jacket and to wear it whenever you dive in open water. Aqualung divers usually purchase an adjustable buoyancy life jacket (ABLJ) which has a refillable compressed air cylinder attached to it and, by the turn of the knob, can inflate the jacket with any amount of air required. This enables the diver to adjust buoyancy on deep dives. But an ABLJ is not only expensive, it is quite heavy so snorkel divers should use a surface life jacket (SLJ). These can have a small CO_2 cylinder attached for inflating in an emergency or they can be inflated by mouth. A surface life jacket is not cheap as it can cost from £25 to £40 whereas an ABLJ can cost from £100 to £250. But when you consider that a life jacket could be responsible for saving your life, it is well worth while saving up for one.

It is unlikely that you will snorkel out to sea too far but there will be times when you are enjoying yourself and will not notice the passing of time.

Therefore a waterproof watch will be useful so that you know how long you have been out.

A diver's underwater compass is important to enable you to maintain a sense of direction and as most divers like to know how deep they are going, they usually have a depth gauge. This need not be expensive as a capillary type depth gauge is quite efficient if washed regularly and looked after.

Another useful item is a 'goodies' bag for collecting specimens or other items as you fin along under water. This could be a nylon mesh shopping bag or even a light weight hessian vegetable sack obtained from your local greengrocer—probably for nothing! There are numerous other items that you could acquire such as a torch, a thermometer, a crab hook, a marker buoy, a whistle, a surface float, etc., but if you had them all, you would go snorkelling looking more like a 'Christmas tree'. In any case, it would become a very expensive sport!

You should purchase the essential items first, and in order of importance. If you purchase a wetsuit and weight belt, the next item should be a diver's knife. A CO_2 life-jacket, an underwater compass and a waterproof torch should also be considered as top priority items for snorkel-diving in the sea, the rest can follow in due course.

Combating Exhaustion and Cold

Exhaustion can be brought on in many ways, mainly, of course, by physical exertion. Other causes are excessive bodyweight, mental tiredness, insufficient sound sleep, panic, smoking, alcohol, water pressure and loss of body heat. Physical exertion is self-explanatory and emphasizes the fact that divers should keep very fit and continually practice. By this means, they will avoid being overweight but a sensible diet is of equal importance. Mental tiredness and worry are often related and can interfere with the pleasure which can be obtained from snorkel diving. Insufficient sleep in a stuffy room with no ventilation often produces headaches and tiredness and, in fact, hypoxia. In the water, diving deeply is quite an effort in itself as the body is subjected to increasing pressures and also there is a gradual loss of body heat. This is not only uncomfortable but results in slower mental reactions with a consequential inability to think clearly, a tightening up of muscles with possible cramp and ultimate unconsciousness.

Whilst it is essential to avoid these causes of exhaustion, it is also necessary to know what action to take should any of them occur. Obviously it is imperative to rest—preferably floating on your back—and to endeavour to control your breathing rhythm with deep, slow breaths. You should, of course, be wearing an inflatable life jacket so inflate it sufficiently to give support while you are resting. Keep calm and consider your circumstances. If the tide is with you, start swimming back to the shore as soon as you have recovered. But if you carelessly forgot to check that the tide would be with you on your return, then you will find it easier to fin either to a spot farther along the coast or to a boat. As a last resort, give the diver's emergency signal and make sure that you hold your arm high out of the water so that it may be easily seen.

A situation like this demonstrates the importance of diving with a buddy. At the first sign of tiredness, be sure to let your buddy know so that assistance can be given. Remember that it is far better to terminate a dive in the interests of safety rather than be foolishly brave so placing not only your own life, but also that of your buddy diver in jeopardy.

Snorkel diving in British waters is never particularly warm and it is wise therefore to wear some form of protective clothing when snorkelling in the sea. A pullover or woollen vest is quite useful as it can provide a certain amount of warmth but offers little protection out of the water when it is wet. The ideal clothing is a well-fitting four piece wet suit. The material used for this is expanded foam neoprene which is actually sheet neoprene containing millions of tiny nitrogen bubbles which provide an insulation barrier between the body and the water. The suit allows a certain amount of water to enter but this is soon heated by the body providing the suit is snug fitting.

A neoprene wet suit not only gives protection but also provides considerable buoyancy. It is necessary, therefore, to wear a weight belt to counteract this buoyancy otherwise it would be extremely difficult to dive under water.

Wet suits are available from numerous reputable manufacturers and are obtainable ready made or made-to-measure. You can also get cut-out kits to make up yourself. The surface of the neoprene can be single or double smooth skin or mesh and in addition, it can be lined with nylon or jersey material to provide strength and ease of dressing. Each of these finishes has its advantages but a 5 mm thick suit with a mesh exterior ('sharkskin') with a nylon lining will probably be found to be the most snag-resistant and comfortable for snorkel diving.

Do not be afraid to make your first wet suit yourself. Not only will it be cheaper but it will give you valuable experience in sticking neoprene together which will be useful if you ever have to repair the suit. The companies who produce wet suit kits supply them with full instructions and will assist you should you encounter any problems. Make sure that you buy a four piece wet suit (jacket, trousers, hood and bootees) as it is important to keep the head, neck and feet warm—even if it means having to buy a larger pair of fins to fit over the bootees.

If you decide to purchase a wet suit kit, you will find that it will include the neoprene, cement, solvent, tape, fasteners and the zip. The neoprene is stuck edge to edge (this is called butt jointing) so make sure that you cover the edges to be stuck together properly with the cement. When tacky, press them together on a flat surface without stretching one edge more than the other. When sticking the arms and legs, use a cardboard roll or milk bottle on the inside and wrap the material round it so that you can press the edges together on a firm surface.

Clean the neoprene surface thoroughly with solvent before cementing the zip into position otherwise the cement will not hold and the zip will pull off. It is advisable to give a double application of the cement to the zip material as it soaks up the cement very quickly. Leave the suit for at least twelve hours before trying it on so that the cement will have time to set properly.

You may not achieve a proper fit at the first attempt and you may have to make some alteration. If this is the case, put the suit on and get a friend to mark the places where material has to be removed. All that has to be done then is to cut the seams, take out the excess materials and restick it.

When you are satisfied that the suit is a reasonably good fit, it is ready for taping—but take your time about this as it can be the most awkward part. The tape has to be well stretched to break up the surface 'skin' and the neoprene surface has to be cleaned with solvent. When you have cut off the necessary length of tape (allow 4 or 5 cm for folding under) wrap it round a bottle or tube before applying the cement otherwise it will curl up and be useless. Apply the cement to the neoprene along the seam to be covered and slightly stretching the tape, attach one end in position then run it down the seam pressing it home with the finger as you go. When you have completed the suit, curb your enthusiasm to wear it for at least two days to give it a chance to set properly and you will not suffer the disappointment of seeing any of the seams come apart when you put it on.

Look after your wet suit and always wash it off in fresh water before hanging it out to dry. You may find it a good idea to leave it in a bath of water overnight to remove all traces of salt. When it is dry, check it for tears or snags and repair them where necessary, then hang it on a padded hanger. If you are storing it for any length of time, sprinkle it with talcum powder or French chalk but do not fold it. A light spraying of silicone grease on the zip and fasteners will prevent them from sticking.

Answering the call of adventure!

The Real Adventure Begins

When you have all the equipment which you think you require, you should be ready for the thrilling experience of snorkel diving in the sea. It is most important that you take the following precautions which will enable you to derive the most enjoyment from the sport:

1. Always dive with a buddy.

2. Make sure that the weather is suitable.

3. Check on the direction of the wind and the tide.

4. Ensure that adequate safety equipment is available on shore.

5. Arrange for warm dry clothing, food and a hot drink on your return.

6. Have a shore lookout prepared to cover all contingencies.

7. Ascertain the proximity of moving vessels in the near vicinity.

8. Ensure that you will not be diving near fishermen.

9. Check all equipment—your own *and* your buddy's.

10. Make sure that you will be able to

get out of the water safely. (Note:—You can usually get in, even from a height, but difficult and slippery rocks, etc. may make your exit hazardous.)

But to make sure that you are always fit for snorkel diving in the sea, keep up your poolwork at every opportunity. If you are in a club or have a group of snorkelling friends, take part in competitive activities such as relay races, games such as dog and bone (similar to the Boy Scouts' game of 'snatch club'), Octopush matches, sharks and dolphins, push-o-war or equipment fitting races—or you may invent some variations of your own.

A group of snorkel divers can organise some marvellous holidays in England as there are many beaches which provide fabulous diving with good underwater visibility. The rugged coastline of Devon and Cornwall is particularly suitable and popular with aqualung and snorkel divers alike.

Many opportunities present themselves to the keen snorkel diver in this vastly different world beneath the waves. The rotting remains of ancient wrecks lay scattered over the sea-bed, many of them close enough to the shore and shallow enough to make them easily accessible to the snorkel diver opening up the exciting prospect of nautical archaeology.

An abundance of large fish including pollack, wrasse, mullet and dog-fish swim lazily through the broad fronds of the thick-stemmed kelp just off the shore, whilst scattered over the sand are the 'flatties'—plaice, sole, skate and turbot. Amongst the rocks and ledges, edible crabs abound and protruding from a hole in the rock can often be seen the twitching antennae of a nervous lobster. Of other marine species, the sea and shore offers a multitude of varieties—starfish, sea-urchins, coral, hermit crabs, shrimps, scallops, scrawny spider crabs, etc.—a never-ending catalogue.

Marine biology is a very interesting hobby, studying and preserving the animals and the plant life from the sea, or even geology—the study of rocks. The next chapter gives you a brief introduction to marine biology which might start you off on your future career. But perhaps the most fascinating and rewarding of all underwater activities is photography. Underwater cameras naturally have to be waterproof and are, in consequence, very expensive but occasionally, a cheap secondhand one can be obtained. Good underwater photographs are in great demand and easily saleable so with care and imagination, you might well be able to earn enough money to buy a new camera. There is no doubt that your interest in the 'silent world' will stimulate you to want to progress and eventually join a branch of the British Sub-Aqua Club. This will enable you, providing you are old enough, to graduate to the aqualung and enjoy the underwater world even more.

An Introduction to Marine Biology

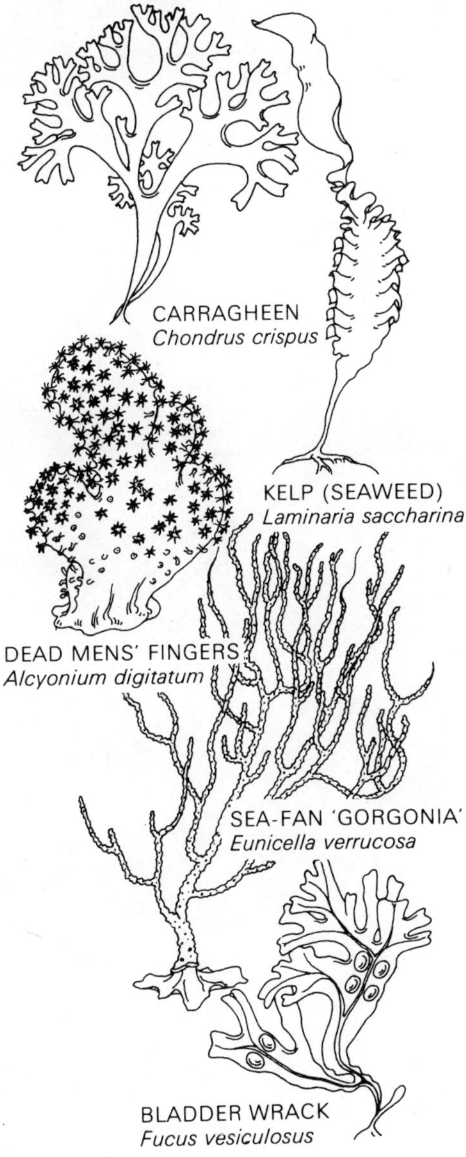

This chapter is intended to give a brief insight into the variety of organisms which abound not only in the sea but also on the sea shore. If it encourages you to appreciate and study marine biology with more awareness of the many wonders of the sea, it will have served its purpose.

The Sea Shore

One of the richest areas of the sea is the sea shore and is best observed by the snorkel diver when the tide is in. Almost every group of marine life is represented including hundreds of varieties of sea-weeds. The sea shore may be of sand, rock, mud or shingle, but we shall mainly consider the first two, for the snorkel diver is more likely to select these for his entry point.

From our point of view, the sea shore may be defined as that area which is neither land nor sea ... or is it both? For approximately half the day, it is exposed to the air, the sun, the wind and the rain and for the other half, it is covered with cold, salty sea water. Therefore it is little wonder that the creatures living there are so different from the more familiar land creatures. For the purposes of marine studies, the sea shore is divided up into zones—the Littoral, the Sub-Littoral and the Supra-Littoral.

The tide reaches highest up the beach at high water (Spring Tide) and this point is often recognisable by a straggling line of sea-weed and is called the Strand Line.

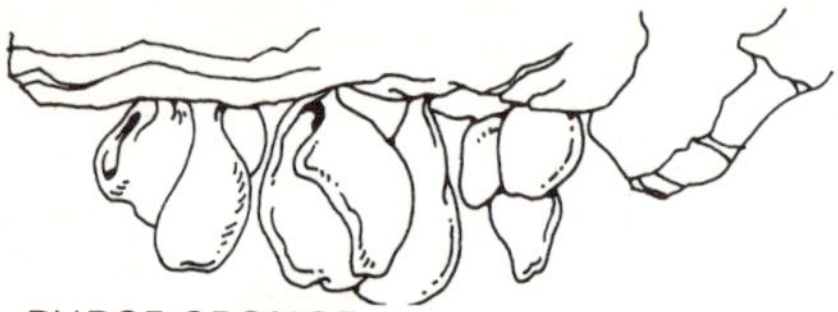

PURSE SPONGE
Grantia compressa

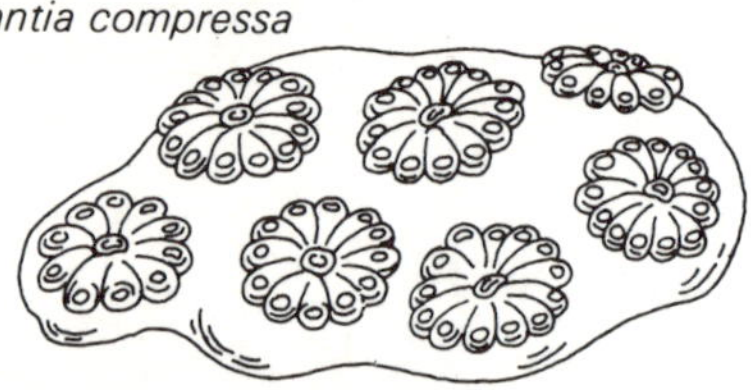

COLONIAL SEA-SQUIRT
Botryllus schlosseri

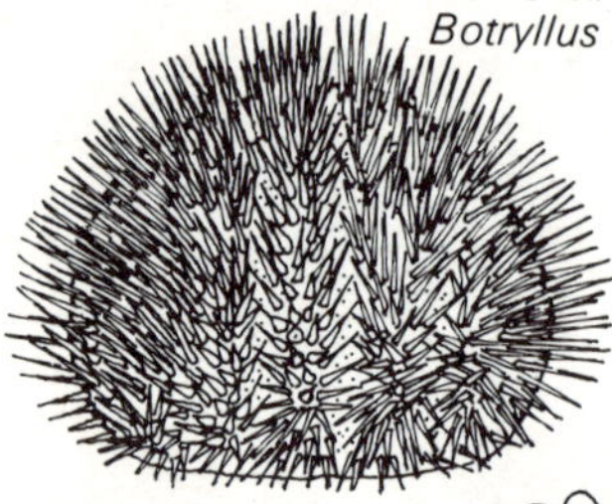

COMMON SEA-URCHIN
Echinus esculentus

DEVONSHIRE CUP CORAL
Caryophyllia smithii

BREAD-CRUMB SPONGE
Halichondria panicea

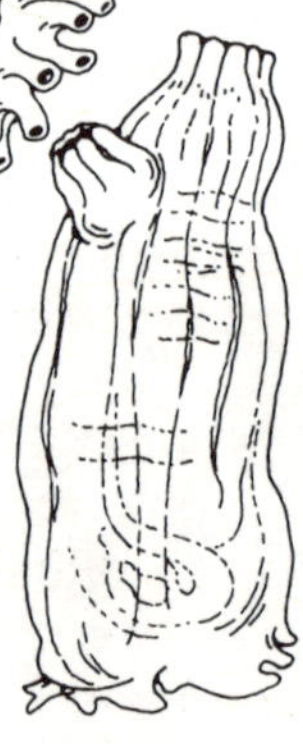

SOLITARY SEA-SQUIRT
Ciona intestinalis

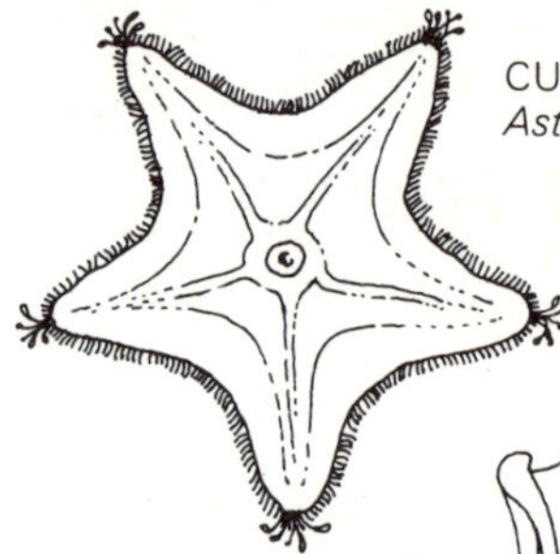

CUSHION STAR
Asterina gibbosa

SEA LETTUCE
Ulva lactuca

BEADLET ANEMONE
Actinia equina

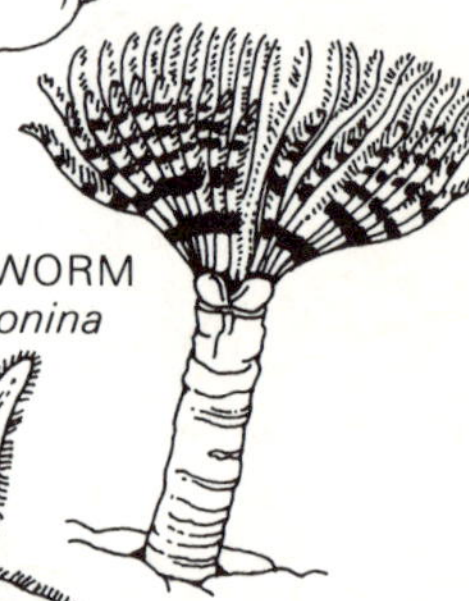

PEACOCK WORM
Sabella pavonina

COMMON STARFISH
Asterias rubens

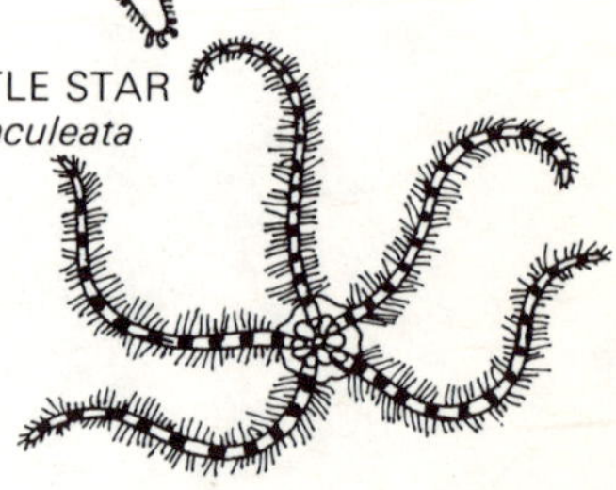

DAISY BRITTLE STAR
Ophiopholis aculeata

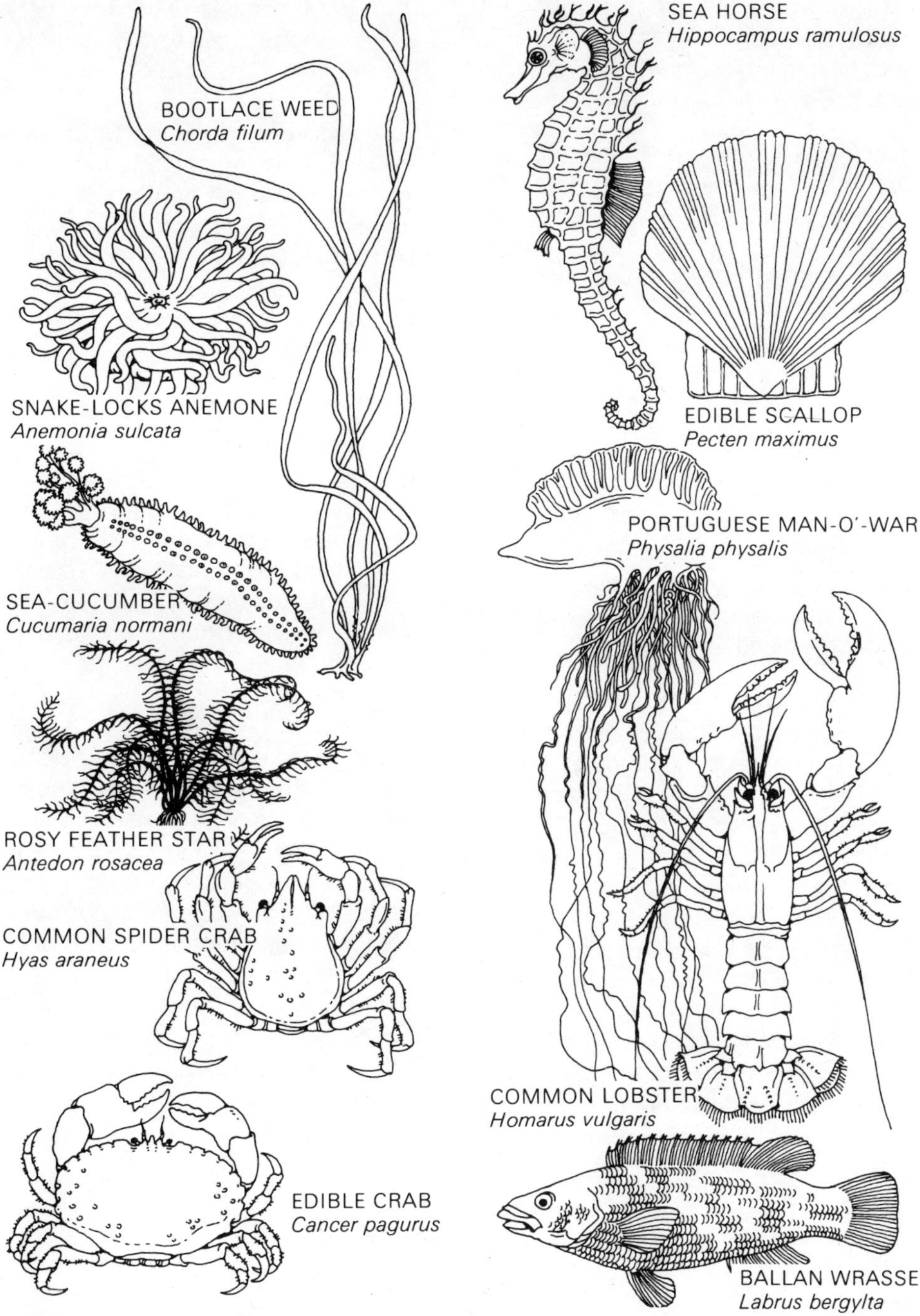
SEA HORSE
Hippocampus ramulosus
BOOTLACE WEED
Chorda filum
EDIBLE SCALLOP
Pecten maximus
SNAKE-LOCKS ANEMONE
Anemonia sulcata
PORTUGUESE MAN-O'-WAR
Physalia physalis
SEA-CUCUMBER
Cucumaria normani
ROSY FEATHER STAR
Antedon rosacea
COMMON SPIDER CRAB
Hyas araneus
COMMON LOBSTER
Homarus vulgaris
EDIBLE CRAB
Cancer pagurus
BALLAN WRASSE
Labrus bergylta

At low water, the sea goes out to its farthest extent but it can only be recognised by the meeting of the sand and the sea for here it leaves no line.

This area, between high and low watermarks, is the true sea shore—the Littoral Zone. Above the high water line (Strand) is the Supra-Littoral Zone and below the low water line is the Sub-Littoral Zone.

The Littoral Zone contains a great variety of organisms which can be observed by anyone who is interested when the tide is out, but when the tide is in, the snorkel diver is able to observe an even greater variety of animals—for this is when the creatures are the most active. Observations may also be continued into the Sub-Littoral zone.

Looking down on to the top of the rocks when snorkelling near a rocky shore may give no evidence of any life at all for this region is subjected to the crashing waves when a rough sea is on the flood (coming in). But in their fight for existence, the marine creatures know better than to expose themselves to the mercy of the sea. Look under the overhanging rocks, under the sea-weed, in crevices, or under the boulders. Here you will find the true world of the marine life—a world abounding in creatures far too numerous to be more than fractionally catalogued.

Marine Life

All organisms can be divided into groups in which each specimen bears certain resemblances to all the others. This is called classification.

The first step is to divide the marine life into plants or animals. The sketches on the previous three pages show the main types of marine plants and animals most likely encountered on the sea shore and within snorkelling distance of the shore.

Sea-weeds

There are numerous kinds of sea-weed, all of which are useful in various ways. Firstly, it is used extensively as a fertiliser in agriculture. It is a very rich source of iodine and is also used in the manufacture of a jelly-like substance called Agar, which is used in large quantities in hospitals and laboratories.

One type of sea-weed called *Chondus Crispus* (Carragheen) is used to make blancmange and in many Welsh coastal towns, one particular type of sea-weed is made into lava bread and eaten with relish. Oriental countries have a very high regard for sea-weed and consider it to be very nutritious as well as extremely low in calories. Considerably more use could be made of this prolific product of the sea because sea-weeds abound in all areas of the sea shore and in the Sub-Littoral zone.

Marine Animals

Porifera—Sponges. The sponges

found on the sea shore are small and will certainly not look like the sponge used in the bathroom. There are several varieties, the common ones being the Purse Sponge and the Bread Crumb Sponge.

As implied by the name, sponges are soft and yielding. They may be various colours such as green, red, yellow or even orange. They are not always easy to find but diligent searching should reap a pleasant reward for these strange little animals are well deserving of a very careful study.

Coelenterates—Jellyfish. These are soft bodied animals varying in size from a few millimetres (e.g. *Aurelia*—common jelly fish) to several metres long (e.g. the Portuguese Man-of-War).

PLANTS

- ALGAE (The Sea-weeds)
  - Green Sea-weeds
  - Brown Sea-weeds
  - Red Sea-weeds
- Flowering Plants
  - Turtle Grasses

ANIMALS

	Group	*Typical Organisms in the Group*
Without a Backbone	Porifera	Sponge, Sea Orange
	Coelenterates	Jelly Fish, Sea Anemone, Coral
	Annelids	Worm, Sea-mouse
	Arthropods	Sub-group: Crustaceans e.g. Crab
	Molluscs	Marine Snail, Octopus, Scallop
	Echinoderms	Sea Urchin, Starfish
Very Primitive Backbone	Tunicates	Sea Squirt, Sea-egg
With a Backbone	Pisces	Fish
	Mammalia	Seal

In this group are also sea anemones and corals—all of which have tentacles. Within the tentacles are stinging cells with which they hold and paralyse their prey. The tentacles contract and draw food towards the mouth which is situated at the centre of the tentacles. Food which is not digested is removed via the mouth.

Although the little stinging tentacles of sea anemones are harmless to humans, they are deadly to little fish. If you put your finger into the tentacles, it will feel tacky. This is due to the little stings, but you will feel no pain whatsoever. However, some jellyfish can cause nasty stings—notably the Portuguese Man-of-War with its dangerous long trailing tentacles.

The jellyfish is in fact, basically, a large sea anemone which floats in the water and hangs upside down with its tentacles trailing. The sea gooseberry is shaped as its name implies and is transparent and jelly-like with two long tentacles. It floats in the water and, being like all jellyfish, a poor swimmer, it is at the mercy of the tides and currents.

Corals are many small anemone-like animals which live together and produce a hard, protective exterior made of calcium carbonate. Dead Men's Fingers is a coral which does not have this hard exterior but is soft and is found in abundance around the British Isles.

Annelids—Worms. Every digger for bait in the sands of the sea shore will know the aggressive Rag Worm (*Nereis*) with its strong black jaws, but the timid Peacock Worm (*Sabella*) which is much more beautiful is often overlooked. *Sabella* lives in the sand on the lower Littoral shore like *Nereis* but makes a long tube for itself which sticks out of the sand some 65 to 100 millimetres. When the tide is out, there is little of interest to see, but when the tide is covering these worms, they begin to feed. This is when *Sabella* is at its most attractive for it extends numerous feathery tentacles which it uses to filter food from the water. The tentacles produce a lovely fan of brown, red or violet hues banded with darker colours. It is remarkable that these beautiful worms are related to the black-jawed *Nereis*, and yet they are very much the same with the exception that whereas the *Sabella* feeds on tiny particles of food and needs a feathery filter to procure it, the *Nereis* feeds on larger tougher food and needs jaws to crush it.

Arthropods—Jointed Legs. A great number of animals fall within this class, many of which are of no interest to snorkel divers and therefore we will concentrate on the sub-group *Crustacea*. These vary in size from the little Pea Crabs about 5 millimetres wide to the large crabs up to 30 centimetres wide.

Usually, crabs have a hard shell of calcium carbonate but the unfortunate Hermit Crab has a soft body and is a tempting source of food for other animals. However, they find a way of coping with their characteristic by making their homes in the empty shells of other animals.

To achieve this, they coil their rear quarters into the empty shell and transport it with them when they move. Unfortunately, as they grow larger, they are forced to leave their temporary home as the shell does not grow with them. Consequently, they are forever seeking a new larger shell and frequently being forced to fight another hermit crab for the right 'to squat'. Barnacles belong to the same group of animals as the crabs. They live in a conical tower of calcium carbonate, permanently lying on their backs. When the sea covers them, they wave their legs in the air and kick food into their mouths.

The Lobster, contrary to popular misconception, is in fact blue during life. It only turns pink when it is cooked. It has two extremely powerful claws and can be between 20 and 50 centimetres long. Rarely is it found close to the shore but usually discovered in a hole in rocks and is only noticeable by the two twitching antennae protruding from the hole—its own built-in detection system.

The Crawfish is bigger than the lobster but does not possess claws so it has to defend itself by shooting backwards out of reach of its enemies by means of its powerful abdomen and tail. Sea Slaters, shrimps and prawns are also *Arthropods* which frequently will be seen by the observant snorkeller.

Molluscs—Marine Snails. These include limpets, mussels, scallops, oysters, winkles, topshells, chitons and the shell-less Mollusc, the sea-slug. Squid and Octopus are also of the mollusc family.

Most of these animals are only capable of a crawling movement over the rocks. They feed on the slimy growths on sea-weeds by licking it off with their rasp-like tongues.

The Scallops however, are capable of more rapid movement. They flap their two shells together and 'skip' along the bottom of the sea bed. Strangely enough, they seem to move in the wrong direction. The reason for this is that water enters the shell through the fringe when the shell opens but when it closes, the fringe clamps tight and seals the gap. Consequently, the water is forced out of the sides at the back of the shell.

Echinoderms—Star Fish. This group also includes Sea Urchins and Sea Cucumbers. Star Fish and Sea Urchins have sucker-like tubular feet by which they move and adhere to the rocks.

Besides these feet, the Sea Urchins also have little stalked pincers about one centimetre long. These are used to pick off debris which might otherwise accumulate on its exterior. It is fascinating to watch a living Sea Urchin and see these pincers in action.

They have a coat of calcium carbonate and if a clean, preserved Sea Urchin is closely examined, individual plates of calcium carbonate can be seen quite clearly.

Sea Cucumbers lie on a sandy bottom looking rather like brown, squat cucumbers and they have fantastic powers (as with other animals in this group) to regenerate lost parts. In fact, if they are irritated sufficiently, they will expel their entire contents and the skin will crawl away and remake all of its lost organs. Fishermen used to regard Star Fish as pests and when brought up in the nets, would cut them in half and throw them overboard. Instead of killing them however, each half would regenerate the lost half thereby doubling the population.

Tunicates—Sea Squirts. These are just like bags with two holes in them. Water goes in one hole and the food is extracted from it, then the filtered water leaves by the other hole. Some Sea Squirts grow close to the rock in a mat-like growth and the rock appears to be studded with small stars. Each arm of these stars is one animal—*Botryllus*—and may be yellow, orange, green, violet or blue. They are the most common of the Sea Squirts and live in colonies.

The *Ciona* however, is a solitary type, brownish and transparent, which grows to some 12 centimetres and is usually seen on pier piles on the lower shore. The inner organs are red and can be seen quite easily.

Pisces—The Fish. These can be divided into two main groups: those that dwell on the bottom (e.g. plaice) and those that live in the main body of the water (e.g. mackerel).

The bottom dwellers or flat fish start life as a normal type of fish with an eye on each side of the head. Eventually, they lie on the bottom on one side and the eye migrates to the upper surface as the fish adopts its bottom dwelling existence. Some fish will lie on their right sides whilst others will lie on their left.

One of the commonest free-swimming fish is the Wrasse—*Labrus*, of which there are numerous colourful varieties. Owing to their bony structure, they are not considered a good source of food.

The intriguing Sea Horse is in fact a fish, but it is seldom seen on the sea shore. It is the strangest fish of all and certainly does not resemble other fish. Unlike normal fish which swim horizontally, the Sea Horse assumes a vertical position in the water and has a coiled tail. The male has the unusual role of looking after the eggs and the newly hatched fish and for this purpose, it has a broad pouch on its tail.

The Importance of Conservation

Although the collection of specimens is a fascinating occupation, it should be stressed that the collection of aquatic specimens by the would-be marine biologist just as souvenirs is to be deplored, as is the wanton destruction of plant and animal life. Many marine creatures have a very slow growth process—in some cases taking very many years to develop. Their collection or destruction by thoughtless people could have far reaching effects on the local marine system. Nevertheless, all snorkel divers should cultivate an interest in the natural history under the sea to get a fuller appreciation of the untold beauty and mystery—so largely unexplored. Learning to snorkel dive correctly is only the beginning. Real snorkel diving begins when you take up the study of marine biology and underwater photography, for both could well be grouped under one heading.

The Preservation of Specimens

Seaweeds—These can be preserved by pressing but as they are often flimsy and feathery, they are difficult to arrange. For successful results, it is recommended that a large tray be half-filled with clean fresh sea water and the mounting paper be placed in it. The mounting paper is that on which it is proposed to display the specimens and a good quality drawing paper should prove ideal. Place the sea-weed in the tray and arrange it as required with a small paint brush. When it is positioned satisfactorily, carefully lift out the paper with the seaweed in place, drain off the excess water and lay it gently on several thicknesses of newspaper. It is preferable to leave the mounted sea weed overnight and then in the morning, cover it with a piece of tissue paper and then layers of newspaper, and press it between two heavy books for about a week. As all seaweeds tend to turn the drying paper mouldy, it is important to change it frequently.

Select a suitable key for identification and mark your specimen with its name and group in indelible ink on the mounting card. This is important as an unlabelled collection is worthless. Details should be given of the date and place where found and any other details which may be important. Who knows, you may have a rare specimen that nobody has discovered.

Animals—Small hard-coated animals such as sea urchins, starfish and crabs can be simply dried outside on a warm, sunny day. the larger hard-coated animals must have their insides removed or preserved. The contents of the sea urchin are easy to remove once the mouth, which is on the underside, has been removed with a sharp knife. The easiest method of removing the spines is to soak the dead animal in a weak solution of bleach for about twelve hours and then to carefully scrub them off. Extreme care is needed for the bleach makes the shell very brittle and easily broken.

It is difficult to remove the contents of the Starfish so they must be preserved. One way to do this is to inject them with 70 per cent alcohol when they are dead, but as this may be difficult and expensive to obtain, Formalin may be used instead. This should be diluted with 90 to 95 per cent sea water. the same solution may be used for soft bodied animals such as sea anemones but these should be totally immersed in the solution.

Organisms which may retract into their shells like the winkle, must be treated differently. They should be placed in a dish of sea water in a cool, shady place where there is no likelihood of it being knocked during the process. Allow time for the animal to expand and then add a few crystals of magnesium sulphate every ten minutes for about thirty minutes. This solution should immobilise the animal in one to five hours, when it can be removed from the tray and immersed in the solution of formalin.

Corals—It is strongly recommended that specimens of coral should not be collected under any circumstances, owing to the many years of growth involved.

Fish—To obtain the best results when preserving fish, they should be doped whilst still alive. Sea water fish can be doped by putting into fresh water for a few hours until it is possible to be picked up without protest—use distilled water for fresh water fish. In this condition, it can be painlessly killed by placing it in a solution of 70 per cent Ethyl Alcohol and 30 per cent water. The body should then be injected with a 10 per cent formalin solution and preserved in the same liquid. For sea water fish, of course, make up the solution with sea water.

Formalin is a very cheap preservative and can be purchased from a chemist. It is best to buy it 'neat' and mix up the amount required with nine parts of water to make up the solution at the time you need it. Be very careful to keep your hands well covered and in the event of being splashed on your bare skin with the formalin solution, quickly wash it off with plenty of clean water.

As mentioned at the beginning, this chapter gives only a sketchy outline of marine biology but it is hoped that it is enough to create an interest in the beginner with the possible progression on to much bigger things.

There have been many books written on the subject and the following list is but a few.

Life in the Sea, *Fishes of the World* and *A Guide to the Sea Shore* are all published in the Hamlyn All Colour Series. Although cheap, they are very good 'starters'.
Life on the Sea Shore—MacDonald Junior Reference Library.
Sea and Sea Shore and *Sea Fishes*—Observer Books.
Shell Life—E. Step.
Pocket Guide to the Sea Shore—Collins Guides.
The Young Specialist looks at the Sea Shore—A. Kosch.

Sea Shore Life—E. M. Stephenson.
The Sea Shore—C. M. Young.
Life on the Shore and Shallow Sea—D. P. Wilson.
The Ecology of Rocky Shores—J. E. Lewis.
The Sea Fishes of Britain and North West Europe—Collins Guides.
British Sea-Weeds—C. I. Dickinson.
The Seas—E. S. Russell and C. M. Yonge.
Instructions for Collectors: 4a Insects; 9a Invertebrate Animals other than Insects; 10 Plants—Natural History Section of the British Museum.
A Classification of Living Animals—Lord Rothschild.
The Life Giving Sea—David Bellamy.
The Seashore and Shallow Seas of Britain and Europe—A. C. Campbell.

Ropemanship

The efficient snorkel diver should be fully aware of the importance of ropemanship and should endeavour to become proficient in the uses of knots for various purposes. This is certainly the case for anyone wishing to become an NSC Advanced Snorkeller as it is essential to have a knowledge of the subject. As the snorkel diver will mainly be concerned with the use of ropes in the water, this chapter deals with the most suitable ropes and knots for use in this environment. The original 'natural' ropes, i.e. manilla, sisal and hemp have given way to ropes made from 'man-made' fibres such as nylon and terylene. These two 'man-made' fibres are non-buoyant and if a floating rope is required, polypropylene or polyethylene are used, with the former being about 50 per cent stronger.

For snorkel divers, ropes made from nylon or terylene are the most useful with nylon being almost twice as strong as the 'polys' and about a third stronger than terylene. Both nylon and terylene are very easy to handle and are pliable and durable. Every opportunity should be taken to practise tying the various knots and learning what their particular use is so that it becomes almost an automatic action to select and tie the most suitable knot for any specific purpose. After tying a particular knot on dry land, try tying it in the pool and then under water with your mask off. You will find that if you can acquire a 10 metre length of 10 mm diameter rope, it will be a useful piece of equipment.

The Reef Knot

This knot is of very little use in the water as it easily 'capsizes' (comes undone). Used mainly for tying bandages, reefing and furling sails and also for knotting an arm sling. Only suitable for ropes of equal thickness. Not to be used under water.

The Clove Hitch

A quickly-made hitch for securing a boat's painter to a bollard or ring. It is not very secure as it loosens if the boat is bobbing about in the water. It can be made by dropping the turns over a bollard or by passing the end of the rope round a rung or through a ring.

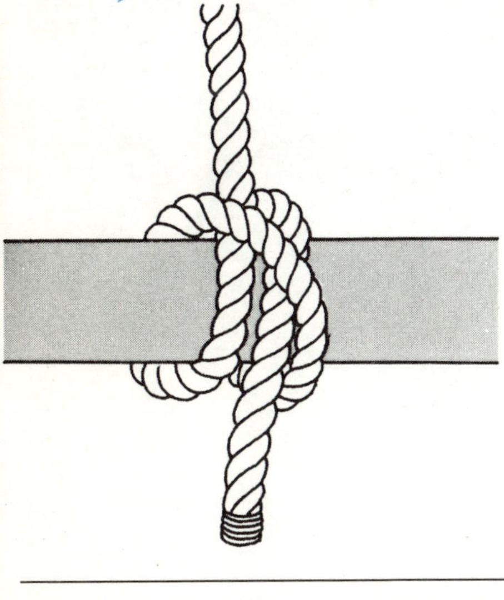

Round Turn and Two Half Hitches

A more suitable knot for use when securing a boat to a bollard. It is more permanent than the clove hitch and easier to undo if the rope is under strain.

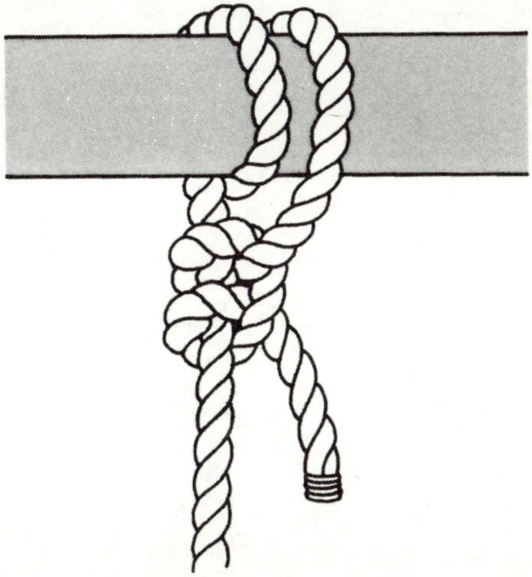

Fisherman's Bend

The tendency for this knot to jam tight makes it an excellent one for securing an anchor. The working end should be made 'secure' by tying with a bowline knot or 'seizing' (i.e. tying the end down with thin twine).

The Bowline Knot

This is by far the most important knot for divers. As it is very unlikely to slip, it is used for securing a body on a lifeline or an object on a rope. It may also be used to make an eye in a mooring line and is ideal for securing a sunken object safely when bringing it to the surface. Divers use it on a rope to maintain contact with the surface during low visibility diving.

The Sheet Bend

Mainly used for joining ropes of unequal thickness. It must be drawn tight to prevent 'capsizing' or made more secure by tying a double knot in the smaller rope.

Sheepshank Knot

Used to shorten a rope without cutting it. It is particularly useful to strengthen a rope which has become chafed and is likely to break (this should only be used as a temporary measure).

Figure of Eight Knot

This is a useful 'stopper' knot tied at the end of a rope. It helps to prevent unreeving and gives a good handhold. It is also quite easy to untie.

Snorkelling Games and Contests

Sharks and Dolphins

This is a game calling for fast manoeuvring in the water. Depending on the number of participants, two or three 'sharks' enter the water with completely blacked-out masks. The rest of the participants are 'dolphins' and the object is for the dolphins to fin as close as possible to the sharks, weaving in and out and diving under without being touched. A dolphin must return to the poolside if touched by a shark. The dolphins must be as silent as possible but any dolphin who hangs about or keeps well clear of the sharks, is ruled out of the game by the umpire. If a shark is grabbed by another shark, the one grabbed calls 'shark' and both swim off in different directions.

After an agreed fixed time, five minutes for example, the sharks are changed and the game continues. A maximum playing time of 20/30 minutes should be played in any one evening. The game improves finning ability, surface diving, lungpower and watercraft.

Push-o-War

This is a team game where two teams position themselves on either side of the pool facing one another. On the command 'go', the opposing contestants enter the water from a 'step-in' and fin as fast as possible towards their opposing number with arms stretched forwards. On meeting, they continue trying to fin forwards to push their opponent feet first towards the side.

Contestants must keep their arms stretched and hands flat against their opponents hands and fin as hard as possible, making sure that they keep pushing in the right direction. If the contestants are evenly matched, they will churn up a lot of water and neither will succeed in pushing the other back. In this case, a time limit must be set and at the end of the period, a draw awarded. This is an excellent exercise for strengthening the legs and improving the finning action.

The game may be played by two opposing contestants at a time or by both teams at once. In the latter case it is best to determine the number of winners required to win the contest.

Snatch Snorkel

Teams face each other as in Push-o-War but with their snorkels inverted (mouthpiece uppermost) in the mask straps and not in their mouths. On the command 'go', the contestants 'step-in' and fin towards their opponent and endeavour to snatch the snorkel without losing their own. They must not touch any part of their opponent or opponent's equipment other than the snorkel.

As soon as a snorkel is snatched, both contestants return to the winner's side of the pool. If after an agreed fixed time some contestants are still trying to snatch their opponent's snorkel, the game is stopped and the winning team is that with the greatest number of snorkels. This is a good exercise for agility and manoeuvrability.

Snatch Fin

This game is similar to Snatch Snorkel but the object is to get one fin from your opponent and return to your side with your opponent and the fin. This is another good exercise for manoeuvrability but also for underwater finning.

Fin Polo

This is played similarly to waterpolo but with all players wearing fins. The game can be varied by only permitting the team defending the deep end of the pool to wear fins. Mask and snorkel should not be used. No physical contact is permitted. Ball may be caught with two hands but thrown with one hand only. Travelling with the ball is not permitted.

Dog and Bone

Two opposing teams face each other across the pool. Each team is numbered off preferably without their opponents knowing the number allocated to each contestant.

An object is placed on the bottom of the pool in the centre and when the umpire calls out a number, both contestants allocated that number 'step-in' and endeavour to retrieve the object and return to their own side of the pool. This is a game which requires quick thinking and good finning.

Relay Races

Many variations of relay races can be devised and are popular with all ages. Snorkel divers should frequently practise normal swimming as well as snorkelling with equipment. It is therefore a good idea to mix swimming relay races with snorkelling relays as it is often said that a snorkel diver forgets how to swim if he is always using his gear. This is true to a point—and certainly, a snorkel diver could get out of practice which could be dangerous if he had the misfortune to lose his fins on a dive in the sea.

A particularly good relay race for keeping in trim is an equipment fitting contest. In this race, all equipment is thrown into the pool and contestants have to retrieve and fit their own gear and fin two lengths. Many variations can be made of this and the more variety that is introduced, the greater the enthusiasm.

Octopush (underwater Hockey)

Octopush originated within the British Sub-Aqua Club and with Southsea Branch in particular. It was first reported in NEPTUNE (now called Diver) in October, 1954, when a dedicated group of members from Southsea decided to originate a game that was as far removed from 'land' games as possible. 'It has now been played at Southsea for the last 30 years although in recent years, the game has been taken up by other clubs and in other countries under different names. In April, 1978 the World Underwater Federation introduced a standardised set of rules and referred to the game as Underwater Hockey. However, there is still a tendency to refer to the game as Octopush in the BSAC and the NSC but although the name may be different, the rules are the same.

Appendix 1

Octopush (Underwater Hockey)

This is certainly the most popular of all sub-aqua competitions and is growing rapidly as an international sport.

The game is played in a swimming pool using mask, fins and snorkel by two teams of six players who try to push a lead puck along the bottom of the pool by means of a small wooden pusher into the opposing team's goal. It is easy to understand its popularity, once tests A, B and C have been passed, anyone can play.

Octopush can be considered an ideal way of furthering training and maintaining fitness amongst trained divers, as well as continuing to improve techniques in basic equipment and get divers thoroughly at home in the water in an enjoyable and exhilarating way. Rivalry between Branches creates links that might not otherwise have been formed. In the winter months Branches will travel miles for a game of Octopush with another Branch. What better way of investigating new diving areas by speaking with divers from these different and far flung places?

The British Octopush Association was formed in 1976 with the following terms of reference: 'The BOA whilst being part of the BSAC is the sole body entirely responsible for all technical aspects, rules and organisation of Octopush (Underwater Hockey) in the United Kingdom.'

SPECIFICATION FOR THE 'SQUID'

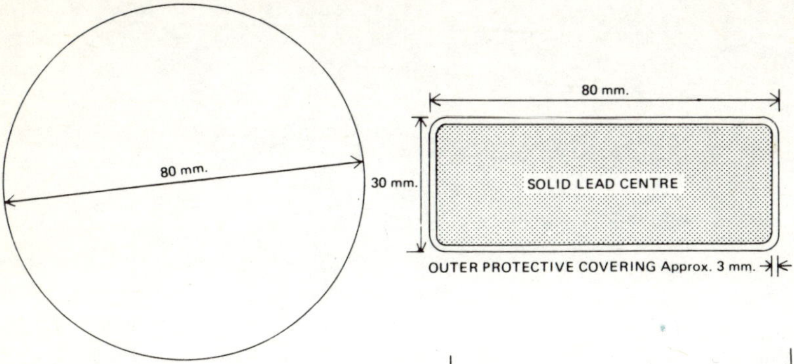

SPECIFICATION FOR THE 'PUSHER'

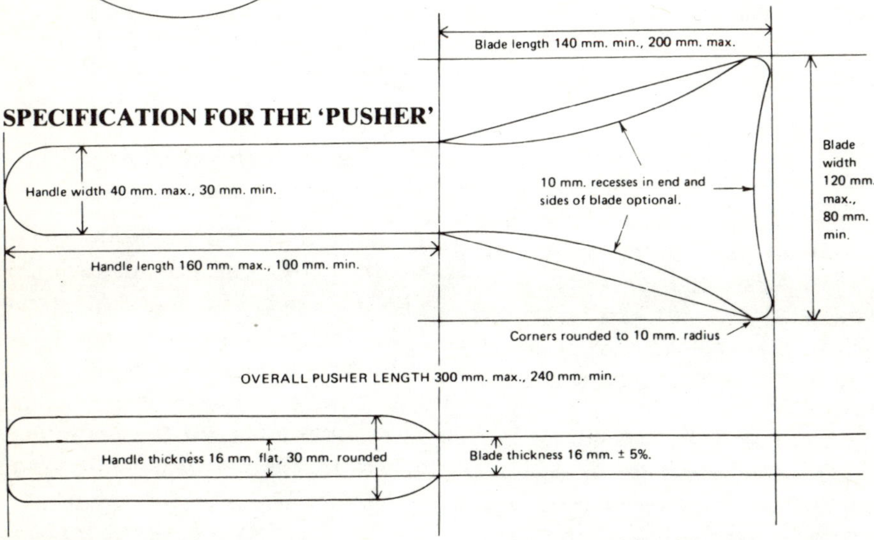

Standard Rules for Octopush

The definitions, specifications and rules which appear in the following, are recognised as the official British Octopush (Underwater Hockey) Rules, by the British Octopush Association, the British Sub-Aqua Club, and through the BSAC the CMAS (the World Underwater Federation), and are valid from 1.9.78.

1. General Dimensions and Equipment Specifications

1.1. The sport of 'OCTOPUSH' is a form of hockey played under water, and it may be played in any swimming pool, or part thereof, the dimensions of which are as near as possible to 25 m long, 10 m wide, and 2 m deep.

1.2. The scoring area is a 'GULLY', and is a depression in the pool bottom against the centre of both end walls, 3 m wide, 12 cm across, and 3 cm deep.

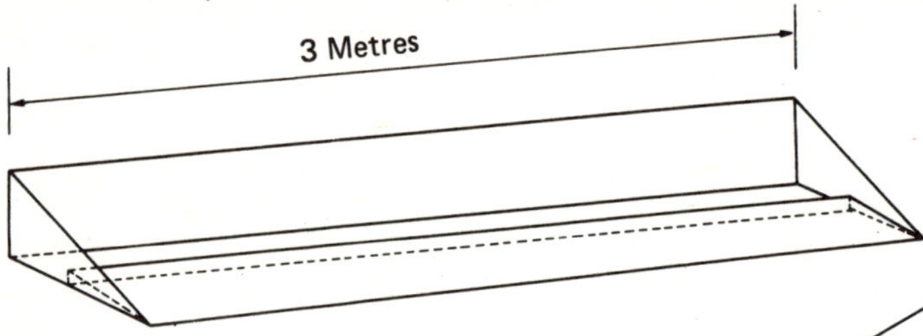

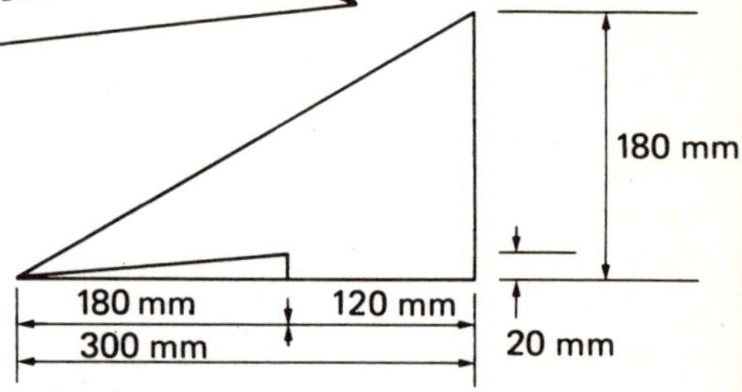

SPECIFICATION FOR THE GULLY FRAME

1.2.1. In pools without this facility the Gully shall be aluminium frames, 3 m wide and placed in the centre of both end walls. (See above) As an alternative the Gullies may also be marked by posts 50 cm high, placed 3 m apart and held to the bottom by suckers or weighs.

1.3. The lead disc employed is a 'SQUID', which is 8 cm in diameter, 3 cm thick, and should weigh approximately 1710 gms $\pm$ 5%.

1.3.1. As a means of protection the squid may be covered by a suitable protective material, provided when finished the overall dimensions conform to those specified.

1.4. The stick used is called a 'PUSHER' and must be made of a buoyant material, i.e. wood, and must conform to the specifications shown in the drawings on page 71.

2. Team Formation and Equipment

2.1. An 'OCTOPUSH TEAM' is composed of 10 members, consisting of 6 players, 2 substitutes and 2 reserves.

2.1.1. For any one match 8 team members must be nominated, only 6 of whom may be in the water at any one time and the remaining 2 wait on the poolside to be used as substitutes.

2.1.2. During the match for which they have been nominated the 2 substitutes may be used to replace any player in the water at any natural break in play, i.e. half-time, or when a goal is scored.

2.1.3. A substitute may also be used in the event of an accident or injury, but only with the approval of the Referee.

2.1.4. Players may not be substituted during the time play is stopped because of an infringement of the rules.

2.1.5. The 2 reserve players may not take an active part in any match they have not been nominated for, but they may become part of the nominated 8 team members prior to the next match, provided other players stand down and in turn become reserves.

2.2. Each player is equipped with a mask, which must have safety glass fitted, a non-metal snorkel, a pair of conventional rubber fins, and a pusher.

2.2.1. Protective gloves may also be worn on the playing hand if required, provided the gloves contain no rigid or sharp reinforcing.

2.2.2. For added safety, it is also recommended that a cap fitted with ear protectors be worn on the head.

2.3. For team identification it is mandatory for the opposing teams to have contrastingly coloured pushers, but they may also be distinguished apart by using constrastingly coloured vests, caps, swimming costumes, etc.

2.4. All equipment used must have the prior approval of the Referee.

3. Officials and their Equipment

3.1. The officials who control an Octopush Match are a REFEREE, two MARSHALS and a TIME-KEEPER/RECORDER, and it is a condition of entry into a match that the decisions of the officials are binding at all times, and in all matters concerning the running of a match the Referee's decision is final.

3.1.1. If required, further officials may be appointed for particular events, but these extra officials will have no direct authority, and will only execute their duties through the Referee.

3.2. The officials shall have available to them the following equipment:

3.2.1. The Referee shall be equipped with a suitable means of creating an audible signal, i.e. whistle, buzzer, gong, bell, etc.

3.2.2. The Marshals shall be equipped with masks, fitted with safety glass, non-metal snorkels, conventional rubber fins and clearly distinguishable T-shirts.

3.2.3. The Timekeeper/Recorder shall be equipped with suitable timing facilities sufficient to time the match and any players sent out of the water for time-penalties, and a means of keeping a written record of the match.

3.3. The REFEREE, whose duties are conducted from a position on the poolside where an uninterrupted view of the playing area can be obtained, is responsible for:

3.3.1. Inspecting all equipment prior to a match.

3.3.2. Instructing the opposing teams of any requirements of the match.

3.3.3. Audibly signalling the starting and stopping of play.

3.3.4. Calling upon each of the opposing captains when ready to commence a match, and awaiting acknowledgement before proceeding.

3.3.5. Acknowledging the Marshal's raised hand when a goal is scored.

3.3.6. Using a casting vote if the Marshals cannot agree on any point pertaining to the match.

3.4. The MARSHALS' duties are conducted from the water and they are jointly responsible for:

3.4.1. Placing the squid at the centre of the pool at any time it is required.

3.4.2. Signalling the scoring of goals by raising a hand until acknowledged by the Referee.

3.4.3. Interpreting foul play and punishing offenders (see parts 5 and 6).

3.4.4. Ensuring that the gully markers are correctly placed at all times.

3.4.5. Signalling 'end of play' to the players under water, on the Referee's signal, by placing a hand over the squid.

3.5. The duties of the TIMEKEEPER/ RECORDER are carried out on the poolside from a position adjacent to the Referee, and may be carried out by one or more persons, or under certain circumstances by the Referee, and the duties are:

3.5.1. To time all playing time and to indicate to the Referee the completion of each time period.

3.5.2. To time any players sent out of the water for time-penalties, and to indicate to the players when they may return to the water.

3.5.3. To maintain a written record of the score, goal scorers, and any other points pertaining to the match on the appropriate match report form.

4. Rules of Play

4.1. A standard 'OCTOPUSH MATCH' will last for 33 minutes, consisting of 15 minutes each way, with a 3 minute break at half-time.

4.1.1. For competition purposes, or if the playing time available for a match is restricted, a shorter time period (minimum 5 min. each way) agreed by the two captains may be played.

4.1.2. The two team captains choose at which end of the pool their team will start by the tossing of a coin, the winner having first choice of ends.

4.1.3. At half-time the teams will change ends.

4.1.4. If it is necessary to have a winning team from a drawn match, 2 extra time periods consisting of 5 minutes each way, may be played.

4.2. The starting positions of the players are: for the 6 players of each team in the water, alongside their respective ends of the pool and in contact with the end by one hand, and for the 2 substitutes of each team, on the poolside at their own team's end of the pool.

4.2.1. At the start, or at any time play is restarted, it is the responsibility of both team captains to signal the Referee their team's readiness by raising a hand, which once acknowledged by the Referee, play will commence.

4.2.2. At the end of play, or should the Marshals wish to stop play for any other reason, they will dive down and place a hand over the squid, this will signify 'end of play', and no further play will take place until restarted by the Referee.

4.3. A match is only said to be 'in play' during the time between the starting and stopping of play by the Referee.

4.3.1. Whilst a match is in play, the squid may be pushed or passed in any direction along the pool bottom anywhere within the playing area by the player in possession.

4.3.2. A player is only said to be 'in possession' whilst the pusher is in contact with the squid.

4.3.3. Any part of the pusher blade may be used to play the squid.

4.3.4. The pusher may only be held by the handle, in either the left or the right hand, but under no circumstances may it be held by both hands simultaneously.

4.3.5. Whilst swimming on the surface players are permitted to use over-arm strokes, but are reminded of the dangers of striking other players.

4.4. A goal is scored when the squid drops into the gully, propelled by or off a pusher, or where posts are used, when the squid passes between them from the direction of the opponents' end.

4.4.1. When a goal is scored, play must stop immediately.

4.4.2. After a goal has been scored the squid is replaced at the centre of the pool by the Marshal.

4.4.3. If any time the squid should enter the gully propelled by anything other than a pusher, it shall be disallowed.

5. Rule Infringements

5.1. Whilst a match is in play, players may be penalised for any rule infringements, including the following:

5.1.1. Handling the squid with the free or playing hand, this includes guiding the squid with an out-stretched finger, but should the squid accidentally touch the back of the playing hand, this will not be considered handling, unless used deliberately to advance the squid.

5.1.2. Lifting the squid off the bottom on a pusher, should it be lifted accidentally it must be immediately dropped.

5.1.3. Standing on the bottom whilst a match is in play.

5.1.4. Grasping another player, or attempting to remove their equipment.

5.1.5. Deliberately impeding or obstructing any other player whilst not in possession of the squid.

5.1.6. Deliberately striking another player with any part of the body or equipment.

5.2. Interpretation of rule infringements is the sole responsibility of the officials.

6. Penalties

6.1. Players who infringe the rules may either be cautioned, or may be obliged to spend, at the discretion of the Marshals, time penalties of up to 2 minutes play out of the water.

6.1.1. Time-penalties do not start until the offending players have left the water and are in the penalty area, which is situated alongside the Timekeeper/Recorder's table.

6.1.2. Timing of time-penalised players is the responsibility of the Timekeeper/Recorder, and the offending players must await a signal indicating expiry of the time-penalty before re-entering the water at the centre line, by sliding gently into the water. Under NO circumstances may a player jump or dive into the water whilst the match is in play.

6.1.3. Players serving time-penalties may not be replaced by substitutes.

6.2. The Marshals can, for persistent infringements, or a particularly bad infringement, dismiss a player from the water for the rest of the match.

6.3. If, in a pool with no wall behind the gully, the squid is knocked out of play by an attacking player, the squid is placed 2 m out from the gully line, 1 m from the side wall, and the match is restarted by the Marshal calling 1 player from each team down to the squid.

6.3.1. If the squid is knocked out of play by a defending player, the squid is placed 3 m out from the gully line in the centre of the pool, and play restarted as above.

6.4. At all times the players will come under the jurisdiction of the officials from the commencement of the match until it is declared ended.

Index